SANTA FE
INDIAN MARKET

SANTA FE
INDIAN MARKET

A HISTORY OF NATIVE ARTS AND THE MARKETPLACE

By Bruce Bernstein

MUSEUM OF NEW MEXICO PRESS
SANTA FE

CONTENTS

INTRODUCTION

Each August, one hundred thousand people attend Indian Market in Santa Fe, New Mexico, the nation's largest and most important Native arts event. The market's one thousand artists, representing 160 tribes, nations, and villages from the United States and Canada, create a sparkling diversity, as do others who come from around the globe to experience the world of Native art and to make and renew friendships. Every imaginable art form is represented, from traditional, cultural-based arts to the avant garde. Indian Market is multigenerational, often with three or four generations in one booth and sixth- and seventh-generation participants. A family that has passed its art from generation to generation might sit beside a university-trained exhibitor.

The longevity and consistency of Indian Market—that it returns year after year—help us understand the relationship of artists to their work over the course of a career, as well as the relationship of the work to artists' families and communities. Indeed, Indian Market is a family reunion, an annual convening of the Native arts and culture world. Today's Indian Market is a remarkable and unique event.

Indian Market's legacy is entwined with Santa Fe; Indian art is iconic to the city, and Santa Fe is the center of the Native art world. Rightly or wrongly, Indian Market is seen as the authority on Indian art. Indian Market holds this position because it is so old and large. It is royalty—the oldest, most distinguished, and most anticipated Indian art fair in the nation.

Indian Market has never bullied its way into the spotlight, however. Rather, it has been a continuous conduit for whatever artists have brought to show, starting in 1922 with Pueblo easel-style paintings and a new kind of pottery from San Ildefonso Pueblo, black-on-black. Over the years, other

SATURDAY MARKET, 1936.

new art forms have been successfully folded into the market. Ironically, these once-new forms are now referred to as traditional art.

When Indian Market began more than ninety years ago, many predicted the demise of Native American cultures; others believed that Indian Market would help preserve Native cultures and provide a means for Pueblo and other Native people to participate in the broader U.S. economy. None could have predicted the way Native arts have since fortified communities, giving new use and values to ancient art forms. The potters and others who participated in the market many years ago created powerful new forms of culture knowledge, which supported and sustained culture at home and, not inconsequentially, served as a vehicle for describing and displaying the persistence, strength, and longevity of Native people to the outside world.

Simplistically, Indian Market puts much-needed funds into communities. But like Native art, Indian Market is so much more. Native art is life—part of the telling, retelling, and renewal of stories that serve to construct and maintain cultural values and principles. Native art provides functionality for an ancient system; modern Native arts have created economic success and, more importantly, cultural persistence and participation. Indian Market proves that art changes lives. Art keeps stories alive, creates new stories, and amplifies those stories for others to hear them.

What follows is a history of Indian Market, assembled from hundreds of interviews, archival sources, and my own participation in Indian Market for more than thirty years. It is a largely chronological history, with three relatively brief chapters describing the forces that set the foundation for the first Indian Fair, as Indian Market was first known.

SETTING THE STAGE

At the turn of the last century, the notion of Indian art as art and not ethnography was in its nascent stages. With the arrival of the railroad and the tourist trade in New Mexico, two thousand years of utilitarian Pueblo pottery making suddenly gave way to the creation of pottery intended for sale to outsiders. Generally speaking, this bourgeoning tourist art reflected a decline in quality. As a counterbalance, the Museum of New Mexico, founded in Santa Fe in 1909, began to encourage potters to make pottery modeled on prehistoric and historic pieces that were thought to represent an unsullied or authentic culture, as determined by curators and anthropologists. Newly made pieces were collected only if they were believed to represent the ceramic lineage of the Pueblo people. Meanwhile, a series of world's fairs, popular in the late

PUEBLO POTTER,
POSTCARD, 1908.

1800s and early 1900s, helped create sympathy for American Indians, then nearly wiped out by Anglo expansion, introduced disease, and the U.S. Indian Wars. At the 1915 Panama-California Exposition in San Diego, Museum of New Mexico director Edgar L. Hewett conceived of a "Santa Fe style" of architecture and envisioned using Santa Fe Fiesta, the city's commemorative celebration of the Spanish reconquest of New Mexico, to promote Santa Fe's appeal as a tourist center.

INDIAN MARKET ARRIVES

By 1922 San Ildefonso potters had developed a new style of pottery, black-on-black, specifically made for sale to Anglos. That year saw the opening of the first Indian Fair, where buyers immediately embraced the new pottery style. The new black-on-black pottery overshadowed curios made for the tourist market and helped counteract the accompanying adverse perceptions of Pueblo pottery. But even with the introduction of new pottery forms and design motifs, Pueblo artists remained faithful to their Native techniques and materials. Remarkable for its modernity, the pottery was neither traditonal nor contemporary. It reflected the ongoing evolution of Pueblo society.

The first Indian Fairs were part of Santa Fe Fiesta and part of Hewett's larger scheme for public anthropology. The fairs were held inside, at the National Guard Armory, and admission was charged. Old pieces (from the museum's collection) and new ones and were displayed side by side. The historical artifacts were intended to illustrate the continuity of tradition, to reinforce the authenticity of newly made objects, to inspire the potters, and to teach buyers and potters what well-made Indian pottery should look like.

All entries were screened and selected by museum staff, who also served as judges, awarding cash prizes. The displays and judging constituted the educational aspect of the fair, intended to teach buyers and potters to differentiate good from bad pottery. The Museum of New Mexico did all the selling; the potters were not present during the sale of their pots. The museum ran Indian Fair until 1926, when the newly formed Indian Fair Committee took over. It carried on fairs under the same formula through 1931.

In 1934 the Indian Fair Committee officially folded itself into the Arts and Crafts Committee of the New Mexico Association on Indian Affairs (NMAIA). All the fair committee members were also members of the NMAIA, so the change was expected. The NMAIA committee struggled with the educational component and organization of the fairs, finally choosing to discontinue fairs in Santa Fe and to move them to the pueblos and reserva-

tions. The new fairs, directed at potters and not buyers, had little success, in part because of an absence of buyers and Anglo admirerers.

In 1936 Saturday Indian markets were created, modeled on Mexican outdoor village markets. As at Indian Fair, cash prizes were given to single out the better pots and potters. But unlike the fairs, artists were allowed to display everything they brought and to sell their own pottery, controlling their interactions with buyers and representing themselves and their villages to the non-Pueblo world. After World War II, however, the markets languished as a small part of Santa Fe Fiesta, stagnating from lack of interest. NMAIA continued hosting the markets more out of habit than desire. Indeed, for several years NMAIA discussed ending the markets altogether.

In the 1960s, increasing national and regional interest in Indian arts and culture created a fertile era for growth. In 1962 Indian Market became a separate event, distinct from Santa Fe Fiesta. By the 1970s, Indian Market had grown in stature and doubled in size and participation each year.

Beginning in the 1980s, Indian Market grew exponentially again. Hundreds of new artists were added in a relatively short period. With such growth, and with many more types of artwork, new rules were needed. When a Northern Plains woman won best of show in 1985, Indian Market permanently shifted its course, becoming broader and less specifically Pueblo and local.

In the 2000s, Indian Market has leveled off at about one thousand participating exhibitors. The rules governing the artwork have increasingly become less formalistic and formulaic. New classifications for art, innovation, and film all guarentee positive growth. Today's Indian Market is unarguably the most important Indian art exhibition in the nation. A weeklong festival, it begins on Monday and continues with cultural and educational programming throughout the week. The market is infused with art world sensibilities; people collect certain individuals' work, artists discuss their work with collectors, and galleries and museums hold myriad exhibitions.

THE MEANINGS OF NATIVE ART

For Native people, art objects are not simply artifacts or pieces of abstraction. They are the embodiment of ancestral origins and often theological markers of action, phenomenon, and explicit record. They serve as catalysts for reconnection with the ancient world and with a specific community as much as they serve as a narrative of the mundane and the extraordinary. Native artists use humor, irony, autobiography, and nuance to voice their thoughts about history, politics, and art. Native art is a form of communication, functioning within and between societies, both Native and non-Native.

Native art plays a central role in health and endurance. The fact that Native people have survived to this day and continue to produce art is itself phenomenal and is a tribute to the power of creative human will and internal strength. Native art is not limited to a focus on the past occupation of lands, social upheaval, and loss; it serves as a catalyst for human activity and cultural

DALIN MAYBEE (SENECA-ARAPAHO)
WITH HIS LEDGER BOOKS, NAMED
BEST OF SHOW IN 2007.

continuity. The arts are an intellectual synthesis of contemporary and immediate experience. Art is why tribes persist, as it strengthens Native American
aspects of life, including performance, word, prayer, and material construction or deconstruction. It holds the message of the past and proposes and sit-
uates the continuity of the individual and Native communities for the future.

As a form of communication, art must and does change. This is as true
for Native art as for other arts, despite an overemphasis on ethnographic
purity. Tradition can be restrictive and stultifying to artists, but it can also
foster creativity. For Native people and their art, tradition is not a stagnant
set of rules and practices but rather a set of principles and values that provide
a foundation for change—a wonderful and vital part of art making, a strength
of Native communities.

The survival of Native people and art is no longer in question. Moreover,
the preservation of Native cultures is once again the task of the Native world
rather than the task of outsiders. *Again*, you ask? Yes, of course. Without
renewal and revival, cultures become more symbolic than functional. They
wither and self-destruct. Native art today serves as a medium to discuss key
issues of personal and community narratives.

SISTER AND BROTHER POSTER
ARTISTS MYLEKA AND TULANE
JOHN (DINÉ), 2011.

SWAIA

Indian Market is planned and presented by the Southwestern Association for
Indian Arts (SWAIA), the descendent of the NMAIA. Some have suggested
that despite SWAIA's preparations and planning, Indian Market "just hap-
pens." If SWAIA were to exit, they say, Indian Market would still take place.
Certainly, some imitator would step in and create an event, but it would be immediately apparent that the history and foundation of the market, as well as SWAIA's
organizational prowess, were missing. Wannabes and has-beens would replace the
quality artists found today down every aisle and in every booth.

At SWAIA, we speak about presenting Indian Market as organizing chaos. SWAIA spends a year planning Indian Market, with attention to every detail except for what constitutes the largest and most significant—what the exhibitors bring. On Saturday morning when the booths open, Indian Market staff are just as engrossed in and dazzled by the displays as everyone else. Planning and organizing aside, it is the art that ultimately makes the show.

POTTER RUSSELL SANCHEZ (SAN ILDEFONSO) AT THE 2006 MARKET.

Official Souvenir Program

of

The Santa Fe Fiesta

and

The First Annual Southwest Indian Fair and Arts and Crafts Exhibition

Santa Fe, New Mexico
September 4th, 5th and 6th, 1922

Given under the Management and Direction of the Santa Fe
Chamber of Commerce and the School
of American Research

CHAPTER 1

"THE HOUR HAS ARRIVED": THE 1922 INDIAN FAIR

═══════════════

MUSEUM OF NEW MEXICO director Edgar L. Hewett opened the first Southwest Indian Fair and Arts and Crafts Exhibition in Santa Fe on September 4, 1922. According to *El Palacio*, the museum journal, Hewett said simply, "The hour has arrived." The fair's stated purposes (1922 Indian Fair exhibition catalog) were:

> the encouragement of native arts and crafts among the Indians; to revive old arts, and to keep the arts of each tribe and pueblo as distinct as possible; the establishment and locating of markets for all Indian products, the securing of reasonable prices; and authenticity of all handicrafts offered for sale and protection to the Indian in all his business dealings with traders and buyers. (1922b)

Participation was organized by tribe. Invitations went out to Southwest Indian agents and Indian boarding- and day-schools principals. No individuals were specifically invited, although a few artists who had worked with the museum, such as Fred Kabotie and Awa Tsireh, were asked to enter work. The Arizona-based Sacaton Indian agent sent a display of Akimel O'odham baskets, and the grand-prize-winning display of Lakota beadwork was sent from the Fort Peck Reservation in Montana. The agency superintendent at Zuni sent jewelry, ceremonial attire, and weapons of offense, while Navajo weavings were sent from the Crown Point and Shiprock agencies. Pottery was entered from San Juan (Ohkay Owingeh), Santa Clara, San Ildefonso, Tesuque, Santo Domingo, Cochiti, Zia, Isleta, Laguna, and Acoma.

The fair was held indoors, at the National Guard Armory on Washington Avenue behind the Palace of the Governors. An admission fee was charged, except to Indian people wearing traditional clothing, whose dress

THE COVER OF THE PROGRAM FOR THE FIRST INDIAN FAIR, 1922.

was encouraged to add local color to the event. The patio of the Governors' Palace was the site of Indian dances and demonstrations of Indian crafts. In his welcoming speech, Hewett spoke of the importance of fostering and preserving Indian crafts in their primitive beauty and cultural distinctiveness, and of the authenticity of the arts and crafts included in the fair.

Francis La Flesche, an eminent ethnologist and Omaha Indian, spoke next. He explained that a movement to revive Indian crafts would help Indian people enter the mainstream American economy. Such a movement would require systematic production, steady markets, and the maintenance of adequate prices. The next speaker, Turine B. Boone, an assistant commissioner from the Bureau of Indian Affairs in Washington, D.C., predicted that reviving Indian arts and crafts would solve "the problem of the Indian" by helping Indians assimilate and become productive citizens. For younger people he advocated attending Indian school and learning a trade. Finally, Tsianina, a Cherokee songstress, sang several songs of her people.

The presence of Boone no doubt was met with some ambivalence. The federal government had recently issued orders prohibiting Indian dance on all reservations and any display of Indian design, language, or clothing in Indian day and boarding schools. The bureau was also supportive of the Bursum Bill, federal legislation that would have quieted all Pueblo land and water rights.

Indian Fair was part of the Santa Fe Fiesta, a community celebration built around public historic pageantry and designed to bring tourism to Santa Fe. Fiesta pageants took place on the Santa Fe Plaza, while other events took place indoors. Tuesday, September 5, was De Vargas Day at the fiesta. It was named for Diego De Vargas, a Spanish governor who led the reconquest of New Mexico in 1692, twelve years after a Pueblo revolt against Spanish colonialism and oppression. According to *El Palacio*, De Vargas Day included a "Grand Spectacular Street Pageant, reproducing the ceremonies incident to the re-conquest of New Mexico in the public plaza A.D. 1693, celebrated annually since 1712." The pageant reenacted the reentry of the Spanish into Santa Fe following their twelve-year exile.

THE INDIAN FAIR

At Indian Fair, inside the armory, walls were covered with Navajo rugs and watercolor paintings on paper. The Fort Peck Sioux Reservation had sent a collection of older beaded garments for display. Other exhibits displayed eagle feather bonnets, vests, pipe bags, dresses, horse gear, and tables full of pottery. On September 5, the local newspaper, the *Santa Fe New Mexican*, sang the new fair's praises:

It is an exhibit embracing the United States and not merely
the Southwest.

There is a display of curios which never can be seen at a curio
store. And there is much of the educational about the Fair with
drawings and paintings, the needlework and other arts taught the
Indian. Entering the big room one takes a big look—it's an eye full
of barbaric splendor.

There is enough pottery to conceal a band of thieves.... The
Indian loves silver ornaments and they showered the fair with their
finest silver.... The walls are covered with blankets, some large
enough for a ballroom.

The pottery entries were a mixture of newly made pieces and older, historic pieces from the Museum of New Mexico and the New Mexico Historical Society collections. Entries were juried, so that only objects considered
good examples of Indian arts and crafts would be exhibited. The older pots
were intended to model what potters should aspire to, both in technique
and design. Archaeologist and assistant museum director Kenneth Chapman
explained, "It was found desirable to encourage the exhibition of certain heir-

looms which are reminders of arts either vanished or in danger of extinction . . . sure to prove an inspiration to younger workers." The goal was a "linking [of] the art of the present craftsmen with that of their forefathers" (Chapman 1924, 221).

Other than historic or heirloom pieces, all entries were for sale. The economic formula was simple: better-made and better-painted arts and crafts would bring higher prices. Sales would bring much-needed cash into Pueblo villages, helping people become more self-reliant and keeping villages economically viable. The participating artists and craftspeople set their own prices, to which the museum added 10 percent to cover the costs of the fair. Chapman remembered the pricing this way:

Shortly before the opening hour, Dr. Hewett, who had been giving the displays a hurried inspection came to me and said, "Chap, some of the pottery prices are getting out of hand. Tonita Roybal has an ordinary size bowl priced at $12.00! You ought to do something about it." I reminded Dr. Hewett that the San Ildefonso

A DISPLAY OF MARIA AND JULIAN MARTINEZ'S POLYCHROME AND BLACK-ON-BLACK POTS AT THE FIRST INDIAN FAIR, ALONG WITH POTTERY FROM THE MUSEUM OF NEW MEXICO'S COLLECTION.

potters had come a long way since he gave them their first encouragement, and that they knew a lot more about selling than any of us. Then I asked, "Do you know any better way for them to find what the buyers will pay?" (Chapman Papers)

Within a half hour of the fair opening, the bowl in question had sold for $13.20.

INDIAN DAY

Wednesday, September 6, was fiesta's Indian Day, which included speeches, Pueblo dances, the judging of Indian Fair entries, and the awarding of prizes. By waiting until the last day of the fair to give prizes, organizers kept the emphasis on education—keeping the pottery and other arts on view and maximizing what potters and buyers might learn by seeing good-quality pottery. Once awarded, ribbons were displayed with the prize-winning pieces.

Many local potters brought their own work to be displayed at the fair. Traders, Indian agency superintendents, and other Anglos also sent examples of Pueblo art for exhibition. But prizes went only to makers of the pieces; no awards were given to dealers who had entered items from their shops. The fair was specifically designed to cut out the middleperson—to provide financial resources directly to Native people. It was also intended to encourage participants to create unique and high-quality pieces to replace the small and inexpensively made curios then sold by traders. The shifting of authority to curators from dealers was vital to Indian Fair and to the entire project to improve Indian pottery. When Chapman or others spoke of "restoring dignity" and returning pottery to its ancestral state, what they intended was to remove the traders' and curio merchants' influence.

Potters also sold their wares in front of the Museum of New Mexico's fine arts building on the plaza, a practice carried on from previous fiestas. Some complained that this practice diminished the quality of the pottery overall, since anything rejected for exhibition was usually sold by the potter either on the plaza or to a curio dealer.

The judges were a committee of three Anglo men, Kenneth Chapman, Wesley Bradfield, and John DeHuff. Like Chapman, Bradfield was a Museum of New Mexico employee. DeHuff was superintendent of the Santa Fe Indian School. Lansing Bloom, assistant director of the museum, served as superintendent of exhibitions, accepting the entries and paying out prize money.

TROPHIES GIVEN TO THE BEST
EXHIBITS AT THE FIRST INDIAN
FAIR, 1922. LAKOTA BEADWORK
WON THE ALBERT FALL GRAND
PRIZE TROPHY.

PRIZE MONEY

Fair organizers set up a total of sixty-three award categories, including prizes for individuals and for pueblos, and a grand prize for best exhibit. Altogether, prize money totaled $1,018. Generally, a first-place individual winner received $5, and a second-place winner got $3. For tribal displays, awards were $25 for first place and $15 for second place. Part of the prize money, $197, came from interest on a $1,000 bond donated by museum patron Rose Dougan. Santa Fe businesses, including hotels, auto dealerships, drug stores, and curio shops, contributed the additional $821. No doubt, business owners recognized that winners would spend most of their prize money in Santa Fe on groceries and other needs. In some categories, winners got a trophy instead of or in addition to prize money.

On top of $1 to $3 earned for selling a pot, a $3 or $5 prize was a substantial sum in this era. Alfonso Roybal from San Ildefonso Pueblo received $25 for the "best collection of paintings in water color owned and painted by Indians." At a time when paintings usually sold for $.50 to $1, this prize must have been enormously encouraging to him and others, demonstrating that being a full-time artist could be profitable.

Lufina Baca of Santa Clara Pueblo took home $13 in prize money, and Tonita Roybal of San Ildefonso took home $10. The biggest prizewinner for pottery was Maria Martinez, who won $23. Each of these women also earned additional money by selling her pottery. The singling out of individuals for prizes made some potters uncomfortable. Martinez approached Chapman after the fair and made it plain that she wanted no more prizes until the work of other deserving women in her pueblo was recognized.

We can only imagine the enormous pride and satisfaction these women and the other artists shared in having their work and culture appreciated. All had attended Indian schools and been severely taught that their culture had no value and that they must learn to be productive citizens. Certainly these artists and others had sold their work, but it had been as curios at world's fairs, railroad sidings, and street corners. Here was a new undertaking that dignified the creators of art.

Special awards for pottery included the grand prize to Maria Martinez, two prizes for jars over fifty inches in circumference to Martinez and Lufina Baca, and a special prize for a new type of decorated pottery (black-on-black) to Martinez. Tonita Roybal also won a special award of $5 for "large black pottery," presumably also a black-on-black piece.

The museum did not give prizes for new or antique textiles because the judges believed the textiles exhibited at the fair were not aboriginal enough in design or material. For instance, the judges called the Navajo blanket designs

THIS MAGNIFICENT JAR BY MARIA
AND JULIAN MARTINEZ WON A $5
AWARD FOR BEST POT OVER FIFTY
INCHES IN CIRCUMFERENCE AT THE
FIRST INDIAN FAIR, IN 1922. PHOTO
BY BLAIR CLARK.

trader-induced, Oriental-based, and not equal in quality to truer Navajo blankets. However, the Santa Fe Business Men's Association sponsored special textile awards. The Crown Point Agency won $30 for the best exhibit of Navajo blankets, while the Shiprock Agency took second place ($20). Also receiving prizes were Zuni ($15) for ceremonial blankets. Zia and Jemez split the second-place prize in the same category.

A single table of basketry at the fair included Mescalero, Western Apache, Jicarilla, Akimel O'odham, Tohono O'odham, Cochiti, Santa Ana, and Santo Domingo pieces. The basketry entries took the judges by surprise. They had planned for only two awards but ended up giving five. They were particularly pleased with the Puebloan baskets, for which a new "Special Prize for best specimen of basketry from a Pueblo in New Mexico" was created after the fair opened. The Sacaton Agency in Arizona received $35 for the best display of basketry.

In the painting and drawing categories, Fred Kabotie (Hopi) won a $5 first prize, and Velino Shije (Zia) and Alfonso Roybal (San Ildefonso) each received $3 second-place awards. Santana Roybal of San Ildefonso won first prize in the student category for her drawings of pottery designs. Many prize-winners in the painting and drawing categories were students at the Santa Fe Indian School, St. Catherine Indian School, Santa Fe High School, and Pueblo day schools.

THE BABY SHOW

One wildly popular feature of the fair was a baby beauty contest. Kenneth Chapman wrote:

> The Baby Show has grown in importance from year to year, until the committee is forced to consider seriously the problem of staging this popular feature in a theater where hundreds can view the spectacle of a score or more of lusty infants, submitting good-naturedly or battling with all their ancient tribal spleen against the indignity of a thorough examination by experts. (Chapman 1924:223)

The baby contest had an unspoken purpose. Fair organizers used it to medically examine Indian babies and to chart their growth. All the contest judges were physicians. This disguised program was considered a necessity due to the epidemics and high child mortality rates then prevalent in the pueblos. Not only had smallpox and influenza taken their tolls on Pueblo children, trachoma rates among children stood as high as 48 percent in some pueblos. Under the pretense of judging beauty, babies were quickly examined and their numbers recorded in an effort to track health as well as early deaths. (The baby contests were discontinued after 1926 because one of the winners died within the year.)

The baby contests were also intended to demonstrate the benefits of Anglo systems of health and child rearing. Fair organizer Margretta Dietrich explained,

> Most Indian babies start life as magnificent specimens of humanity, healthy, bright-eyed and alert, but few survive their first year. It is not uncommon to find strong, competent Indian mothers who from a dozen births, have succeeded in bringing not more than one or two children to maturity, and the problem of combating this high infant mortality is engaging the attention of the Office of Indian Affairs. The Baby Show is doing much to acquaint the public with the health work now being carried on among the Indians, both by the Government and by private means, and a record of the progress of prize babies will be a valuable source of information in years to come. It concerns also the Indian Fair, for how are Indian arts and crafts to survive if the future craftsmen are not to be spared in larger numbers to carry on? (Dietrich 1952)

THE INDIAN ENCAMPMENT

Coming to Santa Fe in 1922 meant a long horse-drawn wagon trip for Pueblo people. It took a full day to cover the eighteen miles from San Ildefonso to Santa Fe, for instance, and a sunrise-to-sunset wagon ride from Ohkay Owingeh. Not every participant traveled to Santa Fe, however. Displays and entries primarily were sent by Indian agents and school superintendents. Those who made the long journey to Santa Fe no doubt enjoyed camping together, meeting new friends, and seeing old acquaintances. Fair organizers provided everything from tents to food. Fair records also indicate that new foods such as ice cream were very popular.

Fair organizers set up an Indian encampment north of Sena Plaza, probably just north of the armory building. The encampment "from early morn to late at night attracted an orderly crowd of [Anglo] visitors who took deep interest in the domestic life of the Indians as there exemplified," wrote Paul Walter in *Art and Archaeology* (1924:189). Although accommodated by fair organizers, the Indians also faced hostility in Santa Fe. Some businesses would not permit Pueblo people to enter their stores or use their facilities.

DANCES AND DEMONSTRATIONS

Dances were a prominent part of the fair and the larger fiesta. Indian ceremonials allowed fiesta visitors to witness "dances not heretofore given outside of the native pueblos on regular Feast Days," wrote *El Palacio* (1922a). In *Art and Archaeology*, Walter explained that dance performances were seen as both a tourist attraction and as a revival and thus a means of preserving Puebloan religion:

> Some of the ceremonies have never been given before away from
> the pueblo; others had not been seen even there for many years
> past and had been born again under the stimulus of the School of
> American Research [a Museum of New Mexico affiliate] in urging
> the Pueblos to revive and preserve their arts and traditions. (Walter
> 1924:188)

The dancing took place on a stage erected in front of the Palace of the Governors and in the palace patio.

At the entrance to the armory, under a canopy and shaded by screens of evergreens, Navajo and Pueblo artisans demonstrated crafts for visitors. *El Palacio* reported, a "trio of Navajos was engaged in sandpainting, and on the other side Navajo silversmiths were fashioning ornaments, Pueblos were making pottery, Navajo weavers were weaving, and a fifth Indian group was doing beadwork" (1922a). On a kitchen range, Indian girls demonstrated their skills in cooking. (The judges gave awards in only one domestic arts area—for the best strings of chilies.)

Clearly, one intention of the demonstrations was to show that Pueblos and other Indian people were domesticated and "civilized"—willing to assimilate into American society and to learn the necessary skills to maintain a household. Paradoxically, while Indian Fair sought to illustrate that Indian people could rid themselves of their aboriginal ways and become "productive citizens," it also sought to preserve their arts and religious life.

CHAPTER 2

POTTERY FOR THE TOURIST TRADE

———————————————

A CONFLUENCE OF FORCES brought New Mexico's Native people to public consciousness in the late 1800s. Among these, the railroad was foremost. The Atchison, Topeka and Santa Fe Railway arrived in New Mexico in 1878; the line reached Galisteo Junction—eighteen miles from Santa Fe—in 1880. Within weeks, a spur line into the capital city was completed.

The arrival of the rail lines coincided with the conclusion of the period of westward expansion. The West, and Native peoples generally, became part of a nostalgia for America's history and for a landscape that was quickly changing with the rapid industrialization of the country. Jonathan Batkin (2008:23) writes, "By early 1880 Santa Fe had become sleepy. The daily newspaper had suspended printing for two years.... But the Atchinson, Topeka & Santa Fe Railway was making its way through New Mexico, and in early February the branch line from Lamy to Santa Fe was completed . . . and a new boom started. On February 27 the *Santa Fe Daily New Mexican* resumed printing, and in that issue was the first advertisement for a store with retail space devoted to Indian curios."

Most rail passengers who traveled through New Mexico in the 1880s were on their way to California. These passengers, like most Anglo-Americans of this era, likely thought of Indians as dangerous or menacing "savages," best seen from a distance. At this time, the Indian Wars were still being waged; their final episode would take place in 1892 at Wounded Knee in South Dakota. Anglo-Americans were not yet ready to embrace Indians as either American or noble. Most rail passengers stayed on the train or ventured no further than the station.

With the railroad's arrival on the West Coast, Manifest Destiny—the notion that the United States was fated to control North America from coast to coast—had been fulfilled. The United States began a shift from a rural to

SANTA CLARA WATER CARRIERS, C. 1910. POTTERY REMAINED ESSENTIAL IN VILLAGES THROUGH THE EARLY TWENTI-ETH CENTURY. PHOTOGRAPH BY EDWARD CURTIS.

an industrial, urban-based economy. With this switch came the intellectual and social search for an "American identity," as well as a reaction to the impersonalization of industrialization. The result was an intellectual movement embodying a longing for simpler, indigenous values. Concurrently, an explosion of information in the late 1800s—a wealth of written description and pictorial evidence—opened the western natural and cultural landscape as a source of national identity and pride.

MASS PRODUCTION

With the ongoing Americanization of New Mexico, Santa Fe–area Native people had already begun the shift to a cash economy; the arrival of the railroad greatly accelerated this process. Trains brought mass-produced goods such as metal pails, crockery, china, and enamelware to Pueblo people. Increasingly, Indians used cash to purchase goods such as flour, coffee, ammunition, and sugar.

The trains also brought tourists, whose fears about the frontier had begun to give way to curiosity. Anglo-American traders took advantage of this situation to sell Native-made curios to visitors. In developing new markets, traders encouraged Indian artists to make pottery and other items expressly for outsiders. Across the Southwest, Native vendors positioned themselves at railway stations selling souvenirs to tourists.

For the tourist business, Pueblo potters abandoned traditional, time-consuming methods in favor of economies of scale and time. They made many small pots in quick succession, setting them aside for drying and then polishing them all together. Such assembly-line methods, together with the fact that traders purchased in bulk and threw away whatever was too poor to sell, combined to produce the worst possible craftsmanship. Pastes were badly prepared and mixed; pigments were quickly readied and poorly applied, so that the colors soon rubbed off; and pots were regularly either under- or overfired, as well as covered with smudge marks. Potters also experimented with store-purchased inks.

FOUR CHANGES

Pueblo potters changed their wares for the tourist market in four distinct ways: reduction in size, simplification of design and surface finish, pseudo-ceremonialism, and intentional archaism. The first change—reduction in size—made pots more appealing to buyers. Small pots fit better in suitcases

TEWA-MADE SANTA FE SOU-
VENIR, 1910. COLLECTED BY
HERBERT J. SPINDEN.

AN ACOMA KITCHEN, C. 1899,
INCLUDES BOTH INDIGENOUS
POTTERY AND MACHINE-MADE
ITEMS. PHOTO BY ADAM CLARK
VROMAN.

and tight budgets. Tourists who wanted only a memento of a visit were more likely to buy a small pot than a large one.

From the potter's viewpoint, small pots were less time-consuming and easier to make. They could be pinched instead of constructed by the labor-intensive coil-and-scrape method. Large pots needed a lot of time to dry and often cracked during the drying process. Small pots had less of a tendency to crack. If they did, the maker had lost less time and material.

Designs were generally simplified to fit on smaller pots. Such designs were often components or portions of designs normally found on larger pots, perhaps reduced in size and certainly simplified to appeal to a non-Indian audience. Anthropologist Ruth Bunzel (1929:36) reported, "The same motives which are used on full sized [Acoma] water jars are transferred to the diminutive pots made for the tourist trade. The patterns are not reduced in size to conform to the size of the vessel, but fewer [design] units are used."

Designs were also simplified to invoke "Indianness." Non-Indians believed that "primitive art" featured classic, clean lines and forms. The busy, complex

"INDIAN POTTERY AND GODS" POSTCARD FROM J. S. CANDELARIO'S THE ORIGINAL OLD CURIO STORE, C. 1910. CURIO DEALERS SOLD THE EXOTIC ALONG WITH THEIR WARES.

design systems of historic Pueblo pottery did not fit this preconceived notion. Traders and other non-Pueblo people often suggested specific designs that they believed would appeal to people searching for Indian pottery.

Pseudoceremonial pots were intended to appeal to a buyer's sense of spiritual yearning and to a belief that voids in Western spirituality could be filled through Pueblo ceremony. But many of the shapes of pseudoceremonial pots, and the accompanying stories, were more than likely created by pottery dealers. For instance, the Tesuque "rain god," although derived from an indigenous form, may have been designed by Santa Fe trader Jake Gold. In the 1890s, Zuni potters began applying frogs and other water creatures to bowls to create "kiva water pots." Similarly, "medicine bowls" were created for the Anglo yearner out of food bowls. In the Tewa pueblos, sellers often labeled pieces as "from the kiva," "used in the kiva," or "originally intended for the kiva." Most of these appellations were sales pitches to gullible buyers.

Buyers would pay more for an older pot than a newer piece. The older piece came from the past, a time when buyers believed all pottery was more authentic and made for home use. Older pots were also thought to be more pure—more Indian. So pottery makers used intentional archaism, copying shapes, designs, and design elements from older pieces onto newly made pots. Potters at San Ildefonso, for instance, revived the shapes, colors, and designs of seventeenth-century polychrome pottery in the 1880s. Many decades later, Ohkay Owingeh women seeking to enter the pottery market utilized the incised patterning used to make Potsuwi'i incised ware, a type of pottery made in the mid-1550s.

By 1900 all the pottery-making pueblos had reformulated their wares for the non-Indian market. But although made quickly and with less effort, although small and perhaps even with a foreign design, pottery for the tourist market maintained its identity as "Pueblo pottery." With the expanding cash economy and the abundance of new manufactured containers, many predicted the demise of the two-thousand-year-old tradition of Pueblo pottery. However, this was a narrow viewpoint. It was traded great distances in the pre-Europeanized Southwest, and beginning in the seventeenth century commonly found in Santa Fe homes.

THE FRED HARVEY COMPANY

While the railway was responsible for bringing tourists to New Mexico, it was the Fred Harvey Company that put travelers "backstage," very often face to face with southwestern Indian peoples. In 1876 Fred Harvey opened his first restaurant for the Atchison, Topeka and Santa Fe Railway at the Topeka station, beginning his legacy of "civilizing the west by providing railroad passengers and local residents with wholesome food served in a graceful style" (Bryant 1974:113). By 1900 the Fred Harvey Company was the railway's sole purveyor of fine food and lodgings, as well as dining car service.

With architect and designer Mary Colter, the Harvey Company built a series of hotels and eateries. Colter's designs were influenced by Native and Spanish styles intended to reflect the Indian cultures of the Southwest and to capture the Spanish colonial period. Harvey-built hotels included the Alvarado at the train station in Albuquerque, El Ortiz in Lamy, La Fonda in Santa Fe, the Castaneda in Las Vegas, the Fray Marcos in Williams, Arizona, and El Tovar at the Grand Canyon. All the Colter-designed hotels featured Navajo rugs and Pueblo pottery in the public rooms.

To add to the colorful atmosphere, the Harvey Company also gave tourists the opportunity to experience Native peoples, albeit in the constructed environments of Fred Harvey. At the Albuquerque railway station, for instance, visitors disembarked from trains to pass between Indians displaying wares on the platform. Continuing through a museum exhibit, they entered a room with Navajo weavers and silversmiths, California Indian basket makers, and other crafts demonstrators. Eventually visitors were ushered into a salesroom to purchase articles resembling those just seen on display or being made.

At the Grand Canyon in 1905, the Harvey Company built Hopi House, a living museum constructed by Hopi builders. It included a museum room, demonstration areas, a workroom, and a salesroom. The upper floors served as a home for Hopi craftspeople, who also performed songs and dances in the evenings. As scholar Marta Weigle notes (1992:138), "Trackside, in stations, at Harvey Houses, and especially at the Grand Canyon . . . Native peoples were placed in settings that resembled display cases."

CURIO DEALERS

Beginning in the 1880s, the mainstay of Aaron and Jake Gold's store was Pueblo pottery. They purchased pottery from Indians coming to Santa Fe and traveled to villages to make purchases. Once strictly used in Santa Fe households, pottery for the booming tourist trade increasingly became a symbol of nostalgia. Gold's Free Museum included a grocery section, so it is likely that potters traded their wares for goods (Batkin 2008:31–33). Generally new pottery could be purchased for a nickel, while antique or older pottery was priced at $.75 or $1.25; larger older vessels commanded as much as $10.

SANTO DOMINGO TRADERS
BOARDED TRAINS AND SOLD
POTTERY, JEWELRY, AND
OTHER PUEBLO-MADE SOUVE-
NIRS TO PASSENGERS. OTHER
PUEBLO CRAFTSPEOPLE SOLD
WARES TO TOURISTS AT TRAIN
STATIONS. PHOTOGRAPH BY
KARL MOON, 1902.

No conclusive evidence has come to light identifying specific traders' involvement in the commodification or invention of nontraditional pottery forms. More than likely, potters and sellers experimented to determine what did and did not sell.

Jesús S. Candelario, who originally entered the curio business with Jake Gold, established the modern curio business in Santa Fe in 1903 with the opening of the Original Old Curio Store on San Francisco Street. Candelario's business and that of others in Santa Fe coincided with the apex of Indian collecting—the Indian craze—throughout the United States, which began about 1900 and ended with World War I.

"Harvey anthropologist" Herman Schweizer bought thousands of Native-made articles to sell in Harvey Company stores. Schweizer bought hundreds of Navajo rugs at a time, specifying the sizes, colors, and designs he desired. He also bought Hopi kachina dolls, Pueblo pots, and Navajo silver. Because the demand was so great, he encouraged quickly made objects that could be sold for little money. Pottery trinkets came to Schweizer by the barrel; he once wrote to Santa Fe trader Jesús S. Candelario urgently asking for "one barrel of Rain Gods." In a 1914 letter to Candelario, Schweizer requested "200 assorted small pieces of pottery, which we can sell at retail from $.15 to $.25."

Generally, pottery could be difficult to sell as a result of it being difficult to ship and transport because it was fragile. In Candelario's correspondence files, customers often complain of broken merchandise: "The pottery sent . . . but one large piece was broken." Along with Pueblo pottery, Gold's Free Museum in Santa Fe sold blankets and pottery from Mexico, rawhide canteens and shields, Navajo blankets, agates, minerals, cactuses, skins, tarantulas, and hundreds of other natural and cultural objects. Trader Thomas Dozier's 1907 sales brochure included much less pottery than other merchandise. The brochure states:

> Indian pottery will be packed in barrels, packing strictly guaranteed, at $3.00 to $5.00 per barrel. . . . A barrel contains about twenty-four pieces, three large, the remainder medium and small sized pieces. We sell only modern made pottery collected from the Indian Villages of San Juan, San Ildefonso, Santa Clara and Tesuque.

CHAPTER 3

MARIA AND JULIAN MARTINEZ
AND THE POTTERY REVIVAL

WHILE THE CURIO MARKET THRIVED, Edgar L. Hewett and Kenneth Chapman swam against the stream. They encouraged Pueblo potters to make wares based on old styles rather than create souvenirs for the curio market. In 1907, while excavating pottery at the Pajarito Plateau near Los Alamos, Hewett and Chapman approached some San Ildefonso women visiting their husbands employed at the excavations. Hewett wanted them to return to their "ancestral purity" by making pottery of the era that predated Spanish settlement. "The women of the Pueblo, when visiting camp, often held animated discussions as to the vessels from the ruins, and it was suggested to some who were known to be good potters, that they attempt to revive their art, and try to emulate the excellence of the ancient wares," wrote archaeologist Alfred Kidder (1925:13).

Pueblo pottery, a two-thousand-year-old art in the Southwest, had well survived every dramatic change in population and influence, the arrival of the Spanish being no exception. Indeed, Spanish settlers depended on Pueblo potters to make storage jars, cooking vessels, and tablewares for their homes. Potters adapted to this new market as well as to new agricultural crops, such as wheat, that were introduced by the Spanish.

But Hewett viewed Pueblo pottery after 1600 as having been influenced by Spanish and American residents and therefore as no longer wholly Puebloan in content or meaning. In his view, Pueblo pottery had lost what he termed "racial purity." Within this pure pottery, Hewett surmised, also survived the true consciousness or "imperishable record" of centuries of Pueblo society.

Chapman's interest was less about science and more about the universality of design. He sought to organize in a linear sequence how Pueblo pottery had developed, utilizing the notion of moving from simplicity to complexity—the addition of line to create form, as well as the evolution from realism to

A BANDELIER BLACK-ON-WHITE BOWL, C. 1450 (RIGHT), AND A 1913 COPY. EDGAR L. HEWETT BELIEVED THAT BY REPLICATING OLD POTTERY, PUEBLO POTTERS WOULD RETURN TO A "PURER" STATE OF CULTURE THROUGH SUBCONSCIOUS MEMORY. PHOTO BY BLAIR CLARK.

A BOX MADE OF CLAY TAKEN FROM THE ANCESTRAL VILLAGE OF PUYÉ, CREATED BY JULIAN AND MARIA MARTINEZ IN 1909. THE PIECE IS PAINTED WITH AN *AVANYU* (WATER SERPENT) COPIED FROM A ROCK ART PANEL NEAR THE VILLAGE OF TSIRGE. PHOTO BY BLAIR CLARK.

abstraction. But as a trained artist, Chapman was more respectful of the artistic process and never dictated to the potters what to make, as did Hewett.

Hewett asked potters to copy or replicate designs he discovered on the ceramics he excavated, a tactic that stifled creativity. Although a few of the women took the advice and made pots in the old styles, the revival was short-lived. Copying old pots turned out to be a deadening aesthetic. Chapman, on the other hand, worked with the potters as an artist, never intruding into their creativity, only providing encouragement. Chapman did not urge the women to make a specific type of pottery or to use a particular set of technical skills.

MARIA AND JULIAN MARTINEZ

Julian Martinez was one of the laborers on Hewett's archaeological excavations on the Pajarito Plateau, while Maria Martinez was among the women from San Ildefonso who visited the site. Julian, along with other laborers, was something of a cultural historian and preservationist, with "a keen interest in everything they found," wrote Kidder. "They helped us identify many specimens which would otherwise have been puzzling, and their comments on the pottery, and especially the designs, were most illuminating" (Kidder 1925:13). Chapman recalled:

> I had become acquainted with one of the laborers [at the Pajarito excavations], a young man from San Ildefonso who while serving as a janitor at the Museum spent much of his spare time poring over the designs on the Museum's collection of ancient pottery. Soon he acquired skill in copying of them in note books, and as his work progressed, I provided him with government reports containing excellent color illustrations of remarkable prehistoric pottery from Arizona. (Chapman Papers)

AN *AVANYU* ON A ROCK ART PANEL NEAR THE ANCESTRAL VILLAGE OF TSIRGE.

Taken together, Julian (1885–1943) and Maria (1887–1980) Martinez, husband and wife, were the most influential southwestern artists and, arguably, Indian artists of the twentieth century. The name Maria Martinez is synonymous with Pueblo pottery—a sign along the highway once read, "San Ildefonso, Home of Maria Martinez"—and her long, productive life made her the best-known Native artist of the last century.

Maria Martinez was a superb ceramic technician, gathering and mixing her clay; shaping, smoothing, and polishing to perfection; and controlling with precision the outdoor firing of her pottery. She was an innovator, reformulating pottery for the non-Indian Market. Although seated in the traditions of southwestern pottery, her designs and highly polished surfaces were not derived from specific Tewa potting traditions but instead were largely taken from ancestral contexts found in books and museum collections.

CRESCENSIO MARTINEZ AND HIS COUSIN JULIAN MARTINEZ BUILD A KIVA IN THE PAINTED DESERT EXHIBIT AT THE PANAMA-CALIFORNIA EXPOSITION, 1914. PHOTOGRAPH BY JESSE NUSBAUM.

Maria lived her entire life in her village of San Ildefonso, forever dismissing her fame and reminding all that she was a Pueblo woman, nothing more, nothing less—a wife, mother, and member of her community. At the same time, she was urged to sign her pottery for authentication, the first to consistently do so.

Pottery allowed Maria to selectively bring influences from the outside world into her pueblo, and she used the money from pottery sales to support the ceremonial and social life of San Ildefonso. With her unsurpassed artistic and technical skill she gave the Pueblo world the gift of continued vigor to make pottery, while providing the non-Pueblo world evidence of her artistic vision and a glimpse into the Pueblo cosmos as well.

Julian, like his uncle and father, was not satisfied with farming or other traditional men's crafts, such as working with wood or leather. A restless, entrepreneurial spirit made him accessible to the non-Pueblo world and prepared him for employment as a laborer on Museum of New Mexico archaeological excavations, and as a janitor and construction laborer at the Palace of the Governors in Santa Fe. He also spent sixteen months in San Diego building exposition exhibits and participated in the living exhibit.

He was one of the first Pueblo watercolorists, a skill he used to document excavated pottery. His painting style changed little over the years, but it was in pottery painting that he displayed his true artistic genius. Julian demonstrated an ability to construct a modern narrative about his life and that of Pueblo people. Although he investigated and utilized Tewa iconography and that of his pottery mentors Martina and Florentino Montoya, he also

drew inspiration from a broad swath of old and new pottery styles, including Acoma, Hopi, and ancestral wares. His sensitive and transcendent painting style also expressed the humility of Pueblo cosmology, sometimes along with flashes of humor.

Julian's inventive transposition of the *Avanyu* (water serpent) from rock art and private use to made-for-sale pottery marked a profound development still in use by potters today. And, most importantly, it was Julian who rediscovered Mimbres iconography to stunning aesthetic effect on the lustrous black pottery that he and Maria created. Through his combination of pattern and design placement, Julian emphasized the elegance, strength, and emotion of Pueblo pottery.

Together Julian and Maria invented Pueblo pottery for the new circumstances that would confront Pueblo people in the twentieth century. Pueblo people wished to retain their own systems of social order and religion while enjoying modern conveniences. Pottery formed the bridge between these often opposing worlds, bringing money to potters so they could participate in

MARIA MARTINEZ AND HER SISTERS DEMONSTRATE POTTERY MAKING IN THE PATIO OF THE PALACE OF THE GOVERNORS, 1912. PHOTOGRAPH BY JESSE NUSBAUM.

the broader society. But importantly, they did so on their own terms by taking an ancient art form and creating new circumstances for its continuance and revitalization. The revitalization was wholly emic to Pueblo culture; it was a reaching out and opening of their lives and villages to the outside through a carefully constructed and mediated means.

TWO BLACKS POTTERY

Encouraged by Chapman to improve her pottery, Maria Martinez never tried to revive ancient styles. Instead, in a series of steps between 1915 and 1920, she and her husband created an extraordinary body of new work. They worked in a variety of polychrome and black-on-red styles, even combining the two on a few exquisite experimental pieces.

In 1917 Maria and Julian began experimenting with solid black pottery, also known as Kapo black, a style introduced to the Tewa pueblos in the seventeenth century. After perfecting the shape and surface of the black pots, they began to put a single *avanyu*—a horned serpent rain spirit—on their pots. This design, punctuated by rainclouds, carried forward Julian's ideas of pottery as a painting surface or canvas.

They learned that by lowering the temperature during firing, the Kapo black ceramics would retain a highly polished finish. Water jars in this style had been made for 250 years in the Tewa pueblos but never with such perfectly executed form and polish. Being soft due to the low-temperature firing, these pieces would not be serviceable but were successful works of art.

In 1917 Maria sold some of her lustrous blackware to the Museum of New Mexico, which displayed the jars, and in 1919-20 her first two blacks. *El Palacio* noted, "In the Acoma Alcove of the Keresan Gallery of the New Museum [Fine Arts Museum] has been placed an exhibit.... Several highly polished pieces of black ware, in form and luster, are exquisite" (1920b).

It is interesting to speculate why Maria chose black pottery to improve upon rather than polychrome wares. Bluntly, black pottery is less arduous to make than polychrome wares, which include several different types of slips and paints and show any slight imperfections in firing. Black pots, in contrast, require only a single color slip and no additional vegetal paints. And as the pots are black, fire scars do not easily blemish their surface. This is not to suggest that making highly polished black pottery is simple. The choice to perfect black pottery was probably in some ways in response to Anglo ideas that pottery needed to display perfection or mastery of hand over materials

THIS EXPERIMENTAL JAR BY MARIA AND JULIAN MARTINEZ, CREATED IN 1917, COMBINES BLACK-ON-WHITE AND BLACK-ON-RED TECHNIQUES. MARIA SIGNED THE PIECE *POH'VE'HA*, HER TEWA NAME. THE SAME SIGNATURE APPEARS ON THREE OTHER PIECES MADE IN 1917 AND 1918. PHOTO BY BLAIR CLARK.

and technology. Moreover, the Martinezes seemed to have understood how this new style would more easily fit into contemporary decors than would polychrome pottery, which is so immediately and outwardly Pueblo. To this polished blackware Maria and Julian in 1919 added a matte decoration to create the first two blacks or black-on-black ware. *El Palacio* took note of this new style: "The largest black olla is in dull finish with a plumed serpent in luster winding its sinuous form around the entire vessel, the effect being surprisingly impressive" (1920b).

The lustrous black pottery was a wholly new type of Native art—Native fine art. Although seated in the traditions of southwestern pottery, the designs and high-polished surfaces were not derived from specific Tewa potting traditions but rather were reformulated via personal expression for the non-Indian market. The pottery reflected personal, creative ideas rather than a goal of preserving tradition as it represented Native culture.

TAKING CREDIT

In 1917 *El Palacio* wrote, "The San Ildefonso pottery makers are successfully reviving ancient symbols and decoration. Upon the suggestion of Dr. Edgar

L. Hewett, they are also 'super burning' some of the ware, giving it a softness of color, a hardness and clearness of ring, that make it superior to any of the pottery now produced at any other pueblo."

Certainly, Hewett, Chapman, and a host of others have either been given or have taken credit for the pottery revival of the period. The Anglo curators, anthropologists, artists, and writers of Santa Fe believed they were saving or salvaging Pueblo culture from being absorbed into the dominant American society. The Anglo Santa Feans believed themselves to be uniquely authorized to rescue Puebloan culture. But this all ignores the ascendant power of Pueblo pottery. An ancient cultural expression, Pueblo pottery had survived and shifted in manufacture and design whenever large-scale change beset Pueblo people, whether in the collapse of social and religious systems in the twelfth century or with the arrival of the Spanish in the seventeenth century.

It is clear that Kenneth Chapman thought *El Palacio's* hyperbole to be unfounded. On the face of it, the claim that black pottery was "super burned" and was harder than other pottery was false. In fact, lustrous black pottery was made with a lowered firing temperature and was softer. But more importantly, Chapman knew that he and Hewett had nothing to do with the brilliant black pottery that Maria Martinez brought to the museum in 1917.

Whenever Chapman wrote about credit for the Martinezes' invention of black-on black-pottery, he put quotation marks around the word *revival,* instead using the term "alleged revival." He understood that all he and the others had done was open a door. It was the potters—specifically the husband-and-wife team from San Ildefonso—who had taken the initiative and accepted the challenging task of reformulating Pueblo pottery.

CHAPTER 4

THE ROAD TO INDIAN FAIR

THE YEARS AROUND THE TURN of the last century were a heyday for world's fairs celebrating industrial progress. Fairs at Chicago in 1893, Omaha in 1898, Buffalo in 1901, St. Louis in 1904, and San Francisco and San Diego in 1915, as anthropologist Burton Benedict put it, presented a "sanitized view of the world with no poverty, no war, no social problems, and very little nature" (Benedict 1983:5). They also idealized the past, with a good measure of nationalism.

With anthropological exhibitions and living demonstrations, the expositions also helped shape public opinion about Native American cultures. Native people were themselves on exhibit to illustrate the "lower rungs of human civilization" on the evolutionary ladder. At the same time, ironically, the fairs fanned an appetite for things and ways supposedly ancient, exotic, indigenous, and alternative, including those of Native Americans. Through the world's fairs, Native people became objects of interest and admiration as the keepers of an ancient American culture. While anthropological exhibitions described North American tribes, physical anthropology, and anthropomorphism, the fairs' carnival zones featured indigenous people from throughout the world: living exhibitions making arts and crafts and dancing and singing for visitors.

Where southwestern Indian people were included, two groups—the Apaches and the Pueblos—were routinely highlighted and inevitably contrasted. The Apaches were still popularly believed to be the marauders of the West. In contrast, the Pueblos were exhibited as sober, sage artisans; residents from time immemorial of neat adobe towns—the continent's first and most ancient republics. Fascination with the Southwest was everywhere during the Louisiana Purchase Exposition in St. Louis in 1904. "By the time the

MERCHANT JULIUS GANS IN HIS INDIAN ARTS AND CRAFTS BOOTH AT THE 1919 SANTA FE FIESTA.

St. Louis exposition closed . . . the southwestern tribes had become the darlings of the American public," writes historian Robert Trennert (1987:150).

AT THE PANAMA-CALIFORNIA EXPOSITION IN SAN DIEGO, PUEBLO FAMILIES WERE PART OF THE PAINTED DESERT EXHIBIT. AS PART OF THE EXHIBIT, MARIA AND JULIAN MARTINEZ DEMONSTRATED POTTERY MAKING AND DANCED FOR VISITORS. PHOTOGRAPH BY JESSE NUSBAUM, 1915.

THE 1915 PANAMA-CALIFORNIA EXPOSITION

For the 1915 Panama-California Exposition in San Diego, Edgar L. Hewett organized the building of the anthropology exhibitions. Jesse Nusbaum, also a Museum of New Mexico employee, supervised creation of an Indian village named the Painted Desert. Twenty-three Pueblo laborers from the Santa Fe region constructed the buildings. These men and their families also lived in

the buildings as a "living exhibit." Based on enthusiasm for the Indian exhibits in San Diego, Hewett formulated a plan for turning Santa Fe into a tourist center and a showcase for Pueblo culture.

Trained in anthropology, Hewett wanted to preserve Pueblo culture as a sort of "living laboratory" that would provide a better understanding of human culture and its workings. Hewett also wanted to use Native people to test his theories (often based more on fancy than fact) about the ancient Southwest. He believed that Pueblo societies could reveal the origins of a natural order of human civilization—with, in his worldview, Anglos at the top of the ladder. Hewett desired to preserve and restore Pueblo culture because "to feel that all this had perished utterly was well-nigh unthinkable . . . here were the [archaeological] habitations, utensils, works of art—wreckage it is true, but susceptible to restoration and almost perfect interpretation." He continued that in a Pueblo dance could be witnessed exactly what was seen centuries ago in the dance plazas of ancestral villages on the Pajarito Plateau. These forms he called the "imperishable record," and through "these channels of self-revelation . . . lie the avenues of approach to real knowledge of the immaterial world of the Indians" (Hewett 1938:119–120). By producing pure pottery or revitalizing Pueblo dance and song, Pueblo culture's antique origins and meanings would be exposed. Hewett's science would be greatly enhanced if he could view and study the "imperishable record" he believed resided within dance and song. At the same time, Hewett felt, Pueblos could be brought into the modern world via economic improvement. Finally, he saw the Pueblos as a potential tourist attraction—one that would create an audience and support for the museums and anthropology programs he was establishing in Santa Fe.

SANTA FE FIESTA

Hewett hoped to bring his plans into reality at the newly created Santa Fe Fiesta. First known as De Vargas Days, the event was begun in 1911 and held sporadically for several years before becoming an annual event in 1919.

For the 1920 fiesta, grandstands were constructed on the Santa Fe Plaza, and Palace Avenue was closed off with a palisade. Santa Fe artist Will Shuster remembered:

> That year, at Fiesta Time, a high stockade was built of aspen poles extending from each end of the Governors' Palace across Palace Avenue and along the north side of the Plaza. It completely

enclosed the street and the Plaza sidewalk. A long grandstand was erected on the Plaza side facing the Old Palace. Admission gates were placed at each end. It was gay and beautiful inside.

Around the outside of the stockade, peering through the cracks between the aspen poles were the less fortunate children and gente of the town watching THEIR FIESTA. The gaiety was all inside. (La Farge 1959:391)

The principal parts of the Santa Fe Fiesta were Indian dancing and a historical pageant featuring reenactment of Diego De Vargas's reconquest of the city in 1692. (The event can actually be traced to 1712, after Vargas decreed that Santa Fe hold an annual remembrance of the reconquest. The early celebration was likely a religious observance that included the procession of a statue of La Conquistadora—Santa Fe's version of the Virgin Mary—through the city streets.)

Early fiestas were simple and local. On July 4, 1912, the *New Mexican* reported that the event included an opening rummage sale and booths on

THE 1921 SANTA FE FIESTA PARADE INCLUDED A SERIES OF FLOATS DEPICTING THE HISTORICAL SEQUENCE OF NEW MEXICO SETTLEMENT—CARRYING A THINLY VEILED MESSAGE OF PROGRESS AND DOMINANCE BY ANGLO CULTURE. THIS FLOAT, "BEFORE TIME," CARRIES MARIA AND JULIAN MARTINEZ AND TSIANINA, A CHEROKEE OPERA SINGER. SOME OF THE MUSEUM OF NEW MEXICO'S POTTERY COLLECTIONS CAN BE SEEN. THE SHIELDS WERE MADE OF CARDBOARD AND PAINTED BY HOPI ARTIST FRED KABOTIE.

three sides of the plaza. On the northeastern corner of the plaza was the "unique Mexican booth and on the [northwest] corner the Indian Booth." Between them and beyond were food booths and amusements.

Hewett wanted to turn Santa Fe Fiesta into a sort of yearly world's fair, complete with ethnological exhibits. The idea was to interweave "archaeology, history, romance, surrounding pueblos, Indian dances and dramas, Spanish folk songs, and miracle plays and fiestas" in a scenic setting. "Indian music, Indian art, Indian handicraft would become integral parts of such pageantry." And with the "pageant could go an Indian Fair, an exhibit of native handicrafts and arts," reported *El Palacio* in 1918(a). Hewett hoped that through Santa Fe Fiestas, Puebloan people would establish their role as representatives of the city and the region.

ON THE FRINGES

Pueblo people were the principal performers in the early fiestas. In 1911 and 1912, and from 1919 through 1926, Indians demonstrated dances, performed in historic pageants, and sold pottery and other arts on the fringes of Santa Fe Fiesta. At the 1919 fiesta, a "Plaza Market" included the sale of Indian arts by at least one dealer, Julius Gans.

For the most part, Indians' fundamental role at fiestas was to portray themselves—sometimes on their own terms but more often than not on fiesta organizers' terms. For instance, Pueblo people helped reenact the 1692 Spanish reentry into Santa Fe, for which "almost two hundred Indians in war costume emerged from the Palace [of the Governors]" reported *El Palacio* (1924c). Unlike their actual ancestors, these Pueblo warriors were mounted on horseback and wore buffalo horn headdresses and feather bonnets—an Anglo stereotype of Plains tribes and not authentic to Pueblo peoples.

ANOTHER PUSH FOR POTTERY

As Hewett fashioned his plan for an Indian Fair at fiesta, he and Kenneth Chapman were still encouraging Pueblo potters. Their efforts were aided by two art patrons, Rose Dougan and Verra von Blumenthal.

Von Blumenthal and Dougan were part of an increasingly large community of Americans seeking a remedy for industrialized society, especially its impersonal nature and its dehumanizing consequences. They believed that human creativity was being destroyed at the expense of industrialization.

They perceived handcrafted objects, especially those made by preindustrial or "primitive" peoples, as critical to keeping the human creative spirit alive.

A native of Russia, Von Blumenthal had encouraged the handicrafts of Russian peasants. After coming to the United States at the onset of World War I, she founded a Slavic handicraft center in Pasadena, California. She

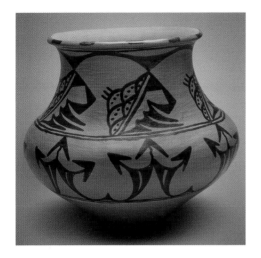 

later visited Santa Fe. Rose Dougan was from Illinois. For several years, she made trips to the Southwest with her sister. Eventually Dougan and Von Blumenthal met. "Rose Dougan . . . became increasingly interested in visiting the modern pueblos, and due to Madame Verra Von Blumenthal's interest and influence, developed increasing interest in stimulating the improvement of pottery production and decoration," wrote Jesse Nusbaum in a letter to the superintendent of Bandelier National Monument many years later. The two women had the financial means to experiment with marketing the pottery being created in the pueblos, particularly that of San Ildefonso.

In 1917 or 1918, Dougan and Von Blumenthal built a summer home at the foot of Tsankawi Mesa, the ancestral home of the Tewa of nearby San Ildefonso Pueblo. They chose the site for their marketing experiment because of its proximity to the pueblo and on the recommendation of Chapman and Hewett. (The San Ildefonso men who built Dougan and Von Blumenthal's home were the same ones who had built the Painted Desert exhibit at San Diego's Panama-California Exposition in 1915 and remodeled the Palace of the Governors.)

Each summer for two or three months, Von Blumenthal and Dougan oversaw and encouraged pottery making at San Ildefonso, hoping to create a better grade of ceramics that could be sold in quantity throughout the United States. Their efforts, in the end, made little impression on pottery production at San Ildefonso, perhaps because of the limited time allowed during summer visits and the limited number of potters—two or so—with whom the women were able to work. Although virtuous, the project was also ill-conceived: two non-Pueblo women could not teach Pueblo woman to make pottery.

Still determined to succeed, in 1917 Dougan and Von Blumenthal turned over $200 to the Museum of New Mexico to create the Pueblo Pottery Improvement Project. According to Kenneth Chapman, the project involved:

1. Inviting potters to submit their wares to Chapman and Bradfield at the museum before offering them for sale elsewhere.
2. Asking each potter to set prices for her pieces.
3. Selecting a few outstanding pieces and explaining why they were chosen (for the quality of form, finish, or decoration).
4. Adding at least 25 percent to the potters' prices for the outstanding pieces.
5. Selling the selected pieces at the museum at a markup sufficient only to repay the School of American Research (SAR; a museum affiliate) for Chapman and Bradfield's time.

The first potters involved in the project were Maria and Julian Martinez. Chapman elaborated:

We [Chapman and Bradfield] set aside four unusually well-formed and finished pieces and asked their prices. Then we commended them for their attractive qualities, and paid 25 percent more than they [Maria and Julian] had asked. That concluded, we told them of our plan and promised even more, for others in their next lot, if they showed further improvement. (Chapman Papers)

Chapman next tried the program with Tonita Roybal, another San Ildefonso potter. She had just completed a disappointing house-to-house tour in Santa Fe, trying to sell two pieces of pottery. "One water jar showed promise, so after praising it . . . I raised her price by 50 percent and asked her to give even more time and thought to her next lot. . . . The result was that within a few months, she was finding a ready sale at three times the price of her former work. That was enough to set things moving in San Ildefonso, for the news soon reached every potter in the pueblo" (Chapman Papers).

The Pueblo Pottery Improvement Project demonstrated that higher-quality pots could be sold for higher prices. The project also demonstrated the need to point out high-quality pottery to both potters and buyers. Selling pottery through the museum succeeded in elevating the higher-quality pots. By extension, rewarding the better pottery told potters that making higher-quality pottery would improve sales.

As part of the Pottery Improvement Project, the new pottery was sold in the museum. Pots were also marked with a small painted bird on their bases to indicate the project's and museum's approval of quality and authenticity. Santa Fe's curio dealers complained about the museum taking their sales. Although a great success, including sales to museums in Cleveland and New York, the museum halted the practice.

FINALLY THE INDIAN FAIR

In 1922 all the threads came together. Spearheaded by Kenneth Chapman, Indian Fair became part of Santa Fe Fiesta. Hewett had foreseen the creation of the fair, but it was Chapman who worked with the potters and painters to create the work that made the fair an instant success. The fair would include the judging of Indian artwork, with Rose Dougan providing a $1,000 endowment to pay prize money to the artists. Most importantly, Maria and Julian Martinez, who had embarked on the creation of a new type of pottery in 1917 and now had found additional encouragement and support, would exhibit pots that would be collected for their beauty as well as their cultural value. They would become the centerpiece of the new Indian Fair.

CHAPTER 5

SANTA FE FIESTA AND INDIAN FAIR: 1923 TO 1926

WITH THE SUCCESS of the 1922 fair, organizers were excited to stage the event the following year. The 1923 *Official Souvenir Program* described the ongoing goals of the fair:

> It was not curiosity on the part of the Santa Fe public, nor a mere desire to attract more tourists hitherwards, that prompted the Fiesta management a year ago to incorporate an Indian arts and handicrafts exhibit as an integral part of its general scheme. The main idea was to impress the Indian mind with the fact that these things, when properly brought before the public, are of far greater value than farm products or a salaried job in carpentry, painting, etc. Almost anybody with a modicum of common sense can raise melons and hoe corn, but only an artist to the manner born can turn out Indian handicraft. So why make a cheap blacksmith out of a boy who can paint a picture that will attract the attention of the whole nation? Above all, by giving him a fair return for his work in this line, make the Indian realize that his arts and handicrafts are wanted, and that people are willing to pay enough for them to make it worth the Indian's while to engage in this line of endeavor. When this is done the question of how to prevent these lines of artistic enterprise from disappearing from the earth will probably be solved. Money talks, and even an Indian has to have a meal-ticket. So, show him where he can market his articles at a fair price, and then, other things being equal, he will come on with the output.

MONICA SILVA, PHOTOGRAPHED IN THE MID-1950s, WAS THE FIRST AND ONLY SANTO DOMINGO RESIDENT TO PARTICIPATE IN THE FIRST INDIAN FAIRS. MARRIED INTO THE VILLAGE, SHE DEFIED THE COUNCILMEN AND JOINED HER SANTA CLARA RELATIVES AT INDIAN FAIR.

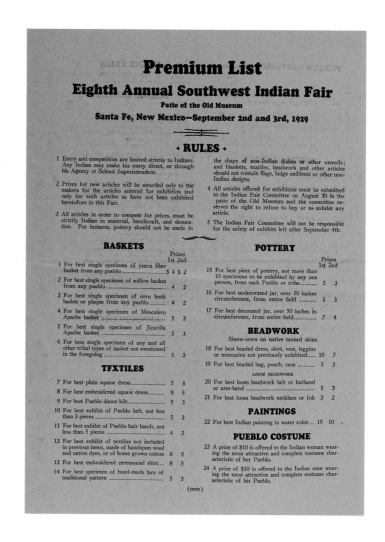

Premium List
Eighth Annual Southwest Indian Fair
Patio of the Old Museum
Santa Fe, New Mexico—September 2nd and 3rd, 1929

• RULES •

1 Entry and competition are limited strictly to Indians. Any Indian may make his entry direct, or through his Agency or School Superintendent.

2 Prizes for new articles will be awarded only to the makers for the articles entered for exhibition and only for such articles as have not been exhibited heretofore in this Fair.

3 All articles in order to compete for prizes, must be strictly Indian in material, handicraft, and decoration. For instance, pottery should not be made in the shape of non-Indian dishes or other utensils; and blankets, textiles, beadwork and other articles should not contain flags, lodge emblems or other non-Indian designs.

4 All articles offered for exhibition must be submitted to the Indian Fair Committee on August 30 in the patio of the Old Museum and the committee reserves the right to refuse to buy or to exhibit any article.

5 The Indian Fair Committee will not be responsible for the safety of exhibits left after September 4th.

BASKETS

	Prizes 1st	2nd
1 For best single specimen of yucca fiber basket from any pueblo	$4	$2
2 For best single specimen of willow basket from any pueblo	4	2
3 For best single specimen of corn husk basket or plaque from any pueblo	4	2
4 For best single specimen of Mescalero Apache basket	5	3
5 For best single specimen of Jicarilla Apache basket	5	3
6 For best single specimen of any and all other tribal types of basket not mentioned in the foregoing	5	3

TEXTILES

	Prizes 1st	2nd
7 For best plain squaw dress	5	3
8 For best embroidered squaw dress	9	5
9 For best Pueblo dance kilt	5	3
10 For best exhibit of Pueblo belt, not less than 3 pieces	5	3
11 For best exhibit of Pueblo hair bands, not less than 5 pieces	4	2
12 For best exhibit of textiles not included in previous items, made of handspun wool and native dyes, or of home grown cotton	8	5
13 For best embroidered ceremonial shirt	8	5
14 For best specimen of hand-made lace of traditional pattern	5	3

POTTERY

	Prizes 1st	2nd
15 For best piece of pottery, not more than 10 specimens to be exhibited by any one person, from each Pueblo or tribe	5	3
16 For best undecorated jar, over 50 inches circumference, from entire field	5	3
17 For best decorated jar, over 50 inches in circumference, from entire field	7	4

BEADWORK
Sinew-sewn on native tanned skins.

	Prizes 1st	2nd
18 For best beaded dress, skirt, vest, leggins or moccasins not previously exhibited	10	7
19 For best beaded bag, pouch, case	5	3

LOOM BEADWORK

	Prizes 1st	2nd
20 For best loom beadwork belt or hatband or arm-band	5	3
21 For best loom beadwork necklace or fob	3	2

PAINTINGS

	Prizes 1st	2nd
22 For best Indian painting in water color	15	10

PUEBLO COSTUME

23 A prize of $10 is offered to the Indian woman wearing the most attractive and complete costume characteristic of her Pueblo.

24 A prize of $10 is offered to the Indian man wearing the most attractive and complete costume characteristic of his Pueblo.

(over)

THE PREMIUM LIST FROM 1929.

The first day of the 1923 Santa Fe Fiesta (De Vargas Day) included the formal opening of the Indian Fair. Music for the event was provided by the Santa Fe Band and the Cherokee singer Tsianina. John DeHuff and Santiago Naranjo, governor of Santa Clara Pueblo, provided the oratory.

The program included dances and music on a stage built in the patio of the Palace of the Governors. Performances included a buffalo dance by Tesuque people, an eagle dance by San Ildefonso, a Comanche dance by Santo Domingo, and an antelope-hunting dance by Cochiti. As in 1922, the 1923 fair was held in the armory. Crafts demonstrators worked both indoors and outdoors. The Indian encampment remained a necessary part of the fair because of the distances between Santa Fe and the pueblos and the participants' lack of cars.

DEMOGRAPHICS

According to *El Palacio*, in 1923 organizers invited about one hundred western Indian schools and agencies to participate in Indian Fair (1923a). Fourteen of these groups ended up sending exhibits. They included the Sells Agency, Southern Pueblo Agency, Pima Agency, Mescalero Agency, Northern Pueblo Agency, Kaibab Agency, Pueblo Bonito Agency, Pipesteam School, Salt River Agency, Navajo Agency at Fort Defiance, Phoenix Indian School, Mount Pleasant School, and Santa Fe Indian School. In addition, Chapman and Bloom extended personal invitations to the governors and councils at Santa Clara and Ohkay Owingeh pueblos. They were probably invited to ensure participation and to alleviate a growing sense of jealousy over San Ildefonso's success at the first fair.

The councils voted on whether or not to participate. In some cases, for instance at Zia Pueblo in 1926, governors and councils refused to allow their people to participate in Indian Fair, wishing to limit contact with and stimulus from the outside world. The Pueblo leaders feared that external influences, especially money, would be divisive, leading to factionalism and disharmony in their villages. Enthusiasm for Pueblo pottery grew. The strength of entries

THE 1925 INDIAN FAIR ORGANIZERS PUT OUT AN EXTENSIVE CALL TO INDIAN SCHOOLS TO SEND STUDENT WORK FOR ENTRY.

and the growing number of potters lessened the need to invite Native people from other parts of the Southwest, let alone other parts of the country.

By 1926 the fair had become primarily southwestern, soliciting exhibitions only from tribes of New Mexico and Arizona. Again invitations went out to the pueblos of Taos, Ohkay Owingeh, Santa Clara, San Ildefonso, Cochiti, Jemez, and Tesuque—to ensure participation in both the fair and in fiesta Indian dances.

CHANGING CALENDAR

In 1923 Santa Fe Fiesta was held Monday through Wednesday, September 3 to 5, but Indian Fair remained open two additional days. In 1924 the fair coincided with the three September days of the fiesta. In 1925 and 1926, the fiesta was moved to August to coincide with Santo Domingo's patron saint day (August 4), honored with a green corn dance. This blatant appropriation was Hewett's suggestion. According to *El Palacio*, he proposed that the Pueblo celebration "be made an integral part of the program," helping to create a "folk festival that would reflect and preserve the distinctive characteristics of Southwestern culture" (1925). In its typical purple prose, *El Palacio* reported in 1926:

> On Wednesday, The Corn Dance at Santo Domingo was magnificent exemplification of what Indian ceremony and drama have been made to mean in Pueblo life. Fiesta visitors by the hundreds made the pilgrimage to Santo Domingo and carried away with them unforgettable impressions.

POTTERY CLEANS UP

In 1923 a total of sixty-one prizes were offered at Indian Fair. That number grew to seventy in 1924 and 1925 and to seventy-two in 1926. Judging categories were broken down by type of art: blankets, baskets, textiles, pottery, beadwork, drawings, painting, and miscellany. Only pottery was further broken into categories by village. A potter would compete only with potters from her own village.

Pottery was far and away the most prevalent art on display and for sale at the fair. In 1926 twenty-three of the seventy-two awards given went to potters. Pottery prize money remained essentially unchanged from 1922, with

IN 1925 AND 1926 HEWETT BEGAN THE SANTA FE FIESTA AND INDIAN FAIR AT SANTO DOMINGO PUEBLO ON AUGUST 4 TO WITNESS THEIR PATRON SAINT CEREMONIES. A SPECIAL TRAIN AND CARAVAN OF CARS BROUGHT PEOPLE TO THE VILLAGE.

INDIAN FAIR EXHIBITS, 1925 OR 1926.

prizes of $5 for first place and $3 for second place awarded in each pueblo. The Santa Fe Chamber of Commerce awarded additional pottery prizes, including $10 for the best collection of Indian pottery (not less than ten pieces) by a single exhibitor or a group of exhibitors from any one pueblo or tribe; $5 for the best undecorated jar over fifty inches in circumference from the entire field; and $7 for the best decorated jar over fifty inches in circumference from the entire field.

In 1923 Maria Martinez won first prize for the "best single specimen of any new type, entire field in competition" for her matte-on-black technique, while Tonita Roybal won the $3 second prize. By 1925 Maria Martinez had eclipsed all other potters at the fair and had "attracted nation-wide attention." In newspaper articles, she was consistently mentioned by name; most other potters were not. By 1925 a clamor was being raised to have potters sign their works, or at the very least to have tags on pieces identifying the makers. The named potter was rising in importance. Names also helped judges award prizes and helped buyers determine good pottery.

CASH FLOW

Exhibitors made a total of $1,400 from arts and crafts sales in 1923. Ten percent of this money went to the museum to pay for fair expenses—leaving $1,260 for the artists. *El Palacio* reported that $385 in sales and prizes were paid to a single potter; this could have been no one other than Maria Martinez (DeHuff). Given that her prize money was only $10 in 1923, she earned more than 30 percent of the $1,260 total in sales money.

Given an average price of $2 per pot, more than six hundred pieces would have been sold during the five days of the 1923 fair. *El Palacio* reported that the fair earned $600 by charging an admission fee of $.50 per person (DeHuff). That averages out to one object sold for every two paid admissions.

Fair revenues in 1924 were $2,506, while expenses totaled $2,597. Organizers spent an additional $2,086 to participate in Santa Fe Fiesta. This money included the cost of bringing approximately seventy-five Pueblo people to Santa Fe for ten days and providing them with camping facilities and food. Indeed, Indian participation was the backbone of the early fiestas. In 1925, out of an $11,000 proposed budget, $5,150, or 47 percent, was paid for Pueblo people's participation.

In 1926 Indian Fair was cut to two days to accommodate the Conquistador's Ball, held in the armory on the final night of Santa Fe Fiesta. Nonetheless, total receipts from the fair were $1,718, including the $.50 admission fees and the 10 percent commission paid to the museum from sales. The expenditures for the fair were $2,567 that year. Pottery sales for 1926 were down from 1925, with about $1,200 paid to artists. The total receipts for the fiesta in 1926 were $13,326. This included $3,550 from sales of 710 tickets at $5 each for reserved seats at the new outdoor Indian Theater.

CROSS-PURPOSES

Increasingly, money was used to validate the success of the fair. "Money talks, and its language is understood even by the red man," reported *El Palacio* (Halseth). While Hewett and Chapman cared about the financial benefits of the fair, they also aspired to the higher purpose of helping to preserve Pueblo cultures.

At the same time, U.S. government policy dictated assimilating Indians into Anglo-American society and even advocated the neglecting of Native cultures. To this end, students were forbidden to use Indian languages at Pueblo day schools and at the Santa Fe Indian School. Classes and curriculum were geared toward training students to work as laborers in the lower rungs of society. Commissioner of Indian Affairs Charles Burke had also issued an anti-dance policy, prohibiting Native dance and song—in essence, Native religion—in Pueblo villages and on Indian reservations.

The Indian Fair, in contrast, allowed Native peoples to participate in the broader society but on their own terms. But by making and selling pottery for the non-Pueblo world, potters also risked backlash from their own pueblos. Some villagers accused them of sharing tribal knowledge with the outside world. Jemez and Santo Domingo were particularly resistant to interaction with the non-Pueblo world. While men's participation in the cash economy was tolerated, women—the potters—were actively discouraged from participating in Indian Fair. In 1926 *El Palacio* reported,

> It was against the wishes of the Pueblo officials that these women [from Santo Domingo] came to the Fair, but last year a third potter risked the wrath of her elders, and after returning from the Fair with money from sales and prizes, and ribbons to prove her success, it may be possible that she scorned their wrath and will come back again next year with several of her sisters. (Halseth)

Pottery sales of course meant more money at the pueblos and thus increased people's acquisition of, and reliance on, non-Pueblo products. Factionalism often resulted. An insular Santo Domingo Pueblo no doubt

frowned upon the introduction of store-bought goods and agricultural products, as well as the acquiring of money to buy them. Pueblo leaders felt that
such products undermined the pueblo's theocracy: if villagers could purchase flour or have wheat threshed and ground outside the pueblo, carefully orchestrated labor and communal work systems within the community
would suffer.

In 1924 fair organizer Odd Halseth made a survey of Jemez pottery
on behalf of the Museum of New Mexico. He found that only two or three
Jemez-born women had learned the art of pottery making, and none of them
had done it since they were young girls. To stimulate pottery making at Jemez,
he provided the women with drawings of designs on old Jemez pottery from
excavations. He wrote in *El Palacio*,

> Everything looked most promising for the rebirth of Jemez pot-
> tery, when an old woman called attention to the fact that there was
> an ancient tradition which prohibited the burning of manure in the
> pueblo from the middle of June until early in the Spring, thus eliminat-
> ing the best season for firing pottery. The cacique [chief] . . . was the
> only person who had power to lift this ban, but he was appealed to
> in vain. (Halseth)

Apparently, someone was willing to defy the religious council:

> But caciques are not as all-powerful among their people as they
> used to be, and that fall one of the Jemez women exhibited at the
> annual Fair in Santa Fe pottery which was fired with manure. The
> following year there were six exhibitions. (Halseth)

The appearance of Jemez pottery at the fair was greeted with great
enthusiasm. In 1924 Leonore Baca received $8 for first- and second-place
prizes for her Jemez pottery, "the first pottery made in 150 years at this
pueblo," according to *El Palacio* (1924c). The lure of money had overcome
traditional prohibitions.

NEW ADDITIONS

In 1924 the Indian aspects of Santa Fe Fiesta received further refinement. Edgar L. Hewett added an event he called House of the Sun. This was an "ancient cycle" pieced together from "fragments of the unique nature drama developed during the centuries preceding the discovery of America by Columbus," according to *El Palacio* (1924a).

The event, consisting of dances by various pueblos, occurred on the second day of the fiesta. Winter animal, hunting, and Shalako dances, as well as summer green corn, basket, and eagle dances, were interspersed with newly created or "revived" dances such as the Braiding of the Peace Belt. This reconstruction necessarily came from the memories of older informants.

With the House of the Sun ceremony, Hewett felt he was accurately reconstructing Pueblo civilization as it had existed about AD 1200. He believed he was assisting in the preservation and revival of Pueblo cultures, as well as providing educational entertainment for fairgoers. The House of the Sun cycle was in Hewett's opinion part of the imperishable record of Pueblo people that if revived would reveal their true values and histories. Hewett desired to test the vitality of Native cultures as well. "The question is what could be done toward the revival of hereditary talents, rendered dormant through several generations of inaction," he wrote (Hewett 1930:146). What was Hewett's motivation? He saw the Pueblos as "living archaeology, nine tenths gone" (Hewett 1923:134). To Hewett and others, the Pueblos were an example of a preindustrial society worthy of preservation for scientific study and tourist curiosity. He had no trouble telling Pueblo people "how to be Indians," because he believed the science of his archaeology provided him with an authority of purpose and knowledge.

Hewett's final fiesta concept to be instituted was creation of an Indian Theater, which he had first envisioned in San Diego in 1915. In 1925 a call went out for a "monumental structure that will be as beautiful as it will be distinctively American, harking back to the days of the Pueblo Bonito and the other great community houses of Chaco Canyon," wrote *El Palacio*. Hewett wrote:

> The Indian deserves an establishment in which to give expression to his unique abilities; not an exotic structure, but a place that would in itself be an expression of his native culture, a place in which he can meet the public, as the artist and teacher that he is fully capable of being. The situation demands a place for performance and a place for exhibition—in short an Indian Theater and an Indian Fair. (Hewett 1925:6)

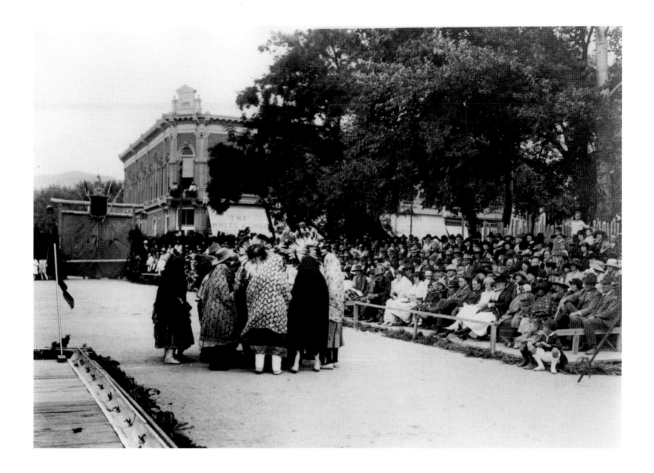

In response, fair organizers carved a bowl-shaped theater with wooden backless bleachers into the hills just north of the plaza. For the 1926 Santa Fe Fiesta, the Indian dances, dramas, and other performances were moved to the theater.

At a dedication ceremony on August 4, 1926, Hewett said the theater was dedicated to "those who came before us." He noted that it should be a celebratory place to honor Indian cultures. He then called upon "our Indian neighbors to produce the first program . . . for we acknowledge that after all these are their mountains and plains and valleys and skies" (Hewett 1926:79–83). Cherokee singer Tsianina then performed an Omaha song, "Song of the Four Hills." Mohawk chief Oskenonton sang "Appeal to the Great Spirit" as he made a fire using sticks. Te Ata (Lakota) recited legends of her people. An eagle dance by San Ildefonso and Tesuque's bow and arrow dance closed the evening.

A DANCE PERFORMANCE ON THE 1921 FIESTA STAGE. MUCH OF THE EARLY FIESTA PROGRAMS WERE NATIVE DANCE PERFORMED BY PUEBLO AND NAVAJO PEOPLE. IN SHORT FIFTEEN-MINUTE SEGMENTS, DANCES PRESENTED A PORTION OF LONGER AND MORE ELABORATE RITUAL.

BACKLASH

Not everyone was pleased with the changes Edgar L. Hewett brought to Santa Fe Fiesta. The city's growing artist community particularly disliked the pompous authority of the Museum of New Mexico and the School of American Research. Others grumbled about the domination of the fiesta by Santa Fe's Anglo population. They said that Hispanic locals were being cut out of the pageantry and celebration.

In 1926 the Santa Fe artist community asserted itself by sponsoring a carnival called El Pasatiempo. The carnival included a Hysterical Parade, a parody of the fiesta's more serious historical pageants. Other events were mock bullfights, a Gran Baile, a children's fête, and the burning of a large marionette called Zozobra or Old Man Gloom, created by Will Shuster and fellow artist Gustave Baumann. The free events were clearly modeled after those of Latin fiestas.

In 1924 *El Palacio* proclaimed that "The Fair has grown in importance year by year until it now stands as a permanent institution which is achieving in every way the great purpose for which it was founded" (1924b). The 1924 fair also assisted in making "notable progress in displacing the nondescript char-

HALSETH PHOTO

Back in My New Mexico!   Pueblo of Santa Clara, with Tsianina and Old Gov. Santiago Naranjo.

POSTCARD FROM 1926 FIESTA AND INDIAN FAIR SHOWING CHARLES LUMMIS, TSIANINA, AND SANTIAGO NARANJO, ALL SUPPORTERS OF EDGAR HEWETT. THIS WOULD BE THE LAST FAIR THEY WOULD ATTEND. THE EXPECTATIONS THAT HEWETT WOULD REGAIN HIS LOCAL STATURE IN THE ARTS AND CULTURE WORLD THROUGH CONSTRUCTION OF THE INDIAN THEATER WERE DAMPENED BY THE CONTINUOUS THUNDERSTORMS THROUGHOUT THE FIESTA AND FAIR.

acter that formerly prevailed in the drawing, designing, and handicrafts as taught the children and substituting therefor a real appreciation of Indian design and workmanship according to the best traditions of the Race," reported *El Palacio* (1924c).

Kenneth Chapman described the 1925 fair as a "great success." *El Palacio* said that the 1926 fair was "on a par with those of preceding years, in spite of the difficulties which the management has experienced in maintaining a systematic program for the encouragement of Indian arts and crafts throughout the year" (1926a).

In 1924 organizers formalized written rules for the fair. Rule 1 stated that entry and competition were limited strictly to Indians. Rule 2 said that prizes would be awarded only to makers of artwork and only to pieces that had not previously been entered in the fair (suggesting that people were attempting to reenter pieces shown previously). Additional rules dealt with the tagging, shipping, and the returning of exhibits to artists. Rule 3 is worth quoting:

AN ARCHERY CONTEST AT THE SANTA FE FIESTA AND INDIAN FAIR, 1925.

All articles, in order to compete for prizes, must be strictly Indian in material, handicraft and decoration. For instance, pottery should not be made in the shape of non-Indian dishes or other utensils; and blankets, textiles, beadwork and other articles should not contain flags, lodge emblems or other non-Indian designs.

As the self-appointed arbiter of "authentic" Native arts, the museum sought to direct changes occurring in the various art forms, imposing its own values in place of those of curio sellers and purporting to be slowing or reversing changes in arts and crafts, returning them to a former level of achievement.

But the written record aside, it is important to understand Pueblo potters' own views on new pottery styles, the pottery market, and their participation in Indian Fairs. Perhaps the immediate success of the fairs was due to an ancient and well-developed strategy for survival—figuring out how to make money without leaving the Puebloan world. As Pueblo scholar Alfonso Ortiz wrote (1994:302), "The Pueblos have traveled and traded widely among one another since far back into prehistoric times and . . . they traded not only material objects but, far more subtly, social institutions and religious knowledge and meanings as well. This pattern of extensive trading and exchange was not so much altered by the Spanish and Americans as it was augmented."

To understand the complexities of Indian Fair, we need to understand that the potters were their own protagonists, choosing to use ancient pottery making as a strategy of survival. Pragmatically, the fairs and pottery were means to make money, but more importantly, they served as a mechanism to share Pueblo culture while strengthening it. In the end, Indian Fairs reinforced cultural values and traditions.

In just five years, the Indian Fairs succeeded in developing an immediate and large audience for new pottery and painting forms. Furthermore, the prize money was significant. No doubt it was a novelty to receive prize money for making pottery or for painting scenes of Native life. It was an ironic enigma to be admired for practicing Native culture, whereas in every other venue, Native people were told that their culture had no value.

Ultimately, fair organizers and audiences developed a growing appreciation of Native people and art. As *El Palacio* explained in 1922, "The white man had sincere admiration for the Indian art and skill and had arrived at some profounder understanding of the Indian viewpoint than he had manifested at any time before" (1922b).

1927 INDIAN FAIR. A PUEBLO
WOMAN WEARING HER FINEST
CLOTHES POSES BY THE FAIR'S
DIRECTIONAL SIGNAGE.

CHAPTER 6

THE FAIR COMMITTEE TAKES OVER: 1927 TO 1931

═══════════════════

IN THE EARLY 1920S, two new entities came on the scene in Santa Fe. The New Mexico Association on Indian Affairs (NMAIA) had been hastily formed in 1922 to fight the Bursum Bill, which would have illegally given an enormous amount of Pueblo land to Spanish and Anglo squatters. The association also fought to protect Indian religious freedoms and to improve health and economic conditions for Native peoples.

Margretta Dietrich was chair of the Indian Fair Committee in 1927 and would continue working with Indian Fair and Indian Market through the 1950s. She began visiting New Mexico in the mid-1920s and in 1929 moved permanently to Santa Fe, where she lived until her death in 1962. She served as president of the NMAIA from 1932 until 1953, when she became honorary president. For many years she served as a tireless advocate for Indian land, water, and human rights. She welcomed Pueblo people needing assistance at her home on Canyon Road. She was also a principal patron of Indian painters, buying nearly 250 works directly from artists and students at the Santa Fe Indian School.

Also in 1922, the Indian Arts Fund (IAF; originally known as the Indian Pottery Fund) was formed to revitalize "the native arts through assembling a representative [pottery] collection . . . and through education of Indian craftsmen by means of that collection." The IAF's founding members included Kenneth Chapman, Wesley Bradfield, and others who had been involved in the Pueblo pottery revival. The IAF purpose was to document Pueblo pottery from 1600 to 1880, clearly in contrast to Hewett, who believed this pottery era was compromised by Spanish influence. The group vowed to save historic pottery by collecting it and making it available for scholars to study and for potters to be inspired by.

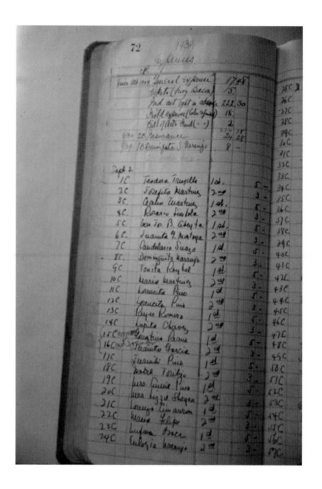

The IAF's major benefactor was oil magnate and philanthropist John D. Rockefeller, who also built the Laboratory of Anthropology to house the pottery collection and to make it accessible for study to scholars and Pueblo people. The collection was designed to show potters that new works of art "can be as excellent as an old one" (IAF 1929) It was hoped that the collection could be displayed at fairs to help educate potters about characteristic designs and to facilitate the creation of more "art and less of ashtrays and trash" (IAF 1929). However, Chapman worried about the safekeeping of the fragile pottery, so he had illustrations of the pottery made instead, and these were circulated in the schools. IAF members also visited pueblos to encourage participation in Indian Fair and to make advance purchases of pottery for inclusion in the fair.

HEWETT DEPARTS

Following the backlash after the 1926 Indian Fair, Edgar L. Hewett removed the Museum of New Mexico from further involvement. Hewett's motivation in creating Indian Fair had been scientific, but by the mid-1920s, his archaeological and public anthropology paradigms were seen as outmoded and paternalistic, and his role as culture and art arbiter in Santa Fe was being usurped by a lively and growing Anglo artistic community.

In 1927 Hewett wrote to a newly formed Indian Fair Committee, "The enlarged program of the School of American Research will prevent its assisting you with the annual Fiesta. . . . Our staff and plant will be taxed to the utmost with the summer school and the research program." But, in fact, Hewett's resignation had little to do with the museum's expanding programs. Rather, he was upset by Rockefeller's rejection of his proposed permanent "Culture Colony," or Chautauqua project, and the artistic community's growing consensus that Santa Fe Fiesta and Indian Fair were largely exclusionary toward local communities. Hewett had done much to establish the Museum of New Mexico and School of American Research, but now academic appointments at the University of New Mexico, University of Southern California, and in San Diego kept him out of Santa Fe for long periods. His building of cultural institutions now complete, he could take a less involved role.

INDIAN FAIR CONTINUES

Although no longer affiliated with the Museum of New Mexico, annual Indian Fairs continued using the formula established in 1922. The fair was juried; all pieces were selected for exhibition by a panel of non-Indian judges. Tables and shelves displaying the artworks were organized by village or tribe. Buyers purchased pieces from the Indian Fair Committee, which then paid the artists. This system provided tight control and has given us records of amounts paid for pots and to artists. As Margretta Dietrich (1952:3) wrote:

> This committee continued the custom of acquiring articles in advance, of passing on all exhibits, brought Indians to the Fair and of deducting ten per cent of the sale price [actually adding 10 percent] to cover some of the expenses. The book-keeping involved was very onerous and the day following the Fair particularly hectic because all the Indians wished their money and unsold goods before returning home.

For the 1927 fair, organizers tried to get potters to sign their works, as noted in the fair literature: "All pottery at the time of purchase should be signed by the maker. This is important for the awarding of prizes." But other than those from San Ildefonso, most potters found this practice unacceptable. Barbara Gonzales, a great-granddaughter of Maria Martinez, suggested that "our own people knew who made the pots" and that "the old-timers never would have thought to sign." Perhaps concealing the names of the potters might also have reduced the factionalism that financially successful pottery was bringing to the villages. In any event, it is interesting to note that financial records of the fairs make it clear that those judging the pottery and writing the awards checks had little, if any, difficulty identifying the makers of the pottery.

Although little specific information is available on the first fair organized by the committee (1927), we do know that local arts patron and Native rights advocate Martha White loaned the committee $500 to cover the costs of renting the hall, building the exhibits, printing prize ribbons, and purchasing pottery in advance. Committee president Dietrich and committee members Amelia White (Martha White's sister) and Mary Wheelwright also made donations totaling $250. The Dougan Pottery Fund was turned over to the committee from the museum to continue the work intended by its donor.

Although we don't know all the prize winners from 1927, the expense book shows that San Ildefonso pottery outsold everything else at the fair that year. San Ildelfonso's Susanna Aguilar won a first-place prize of $5; Maria Martinez won $3 for second place. In addition, Aguilar sold $44 worth of pottery, with most pieces priced from $2.50 to $3. Maria Martinez took home $98.50 from pottery sales. Her husband, Julian, earned $38.50 (presumably from painting sales), and her sisters Desideria and Anna made $53.75 and $23.50, respectively. Lufina Baca of Santa Clara earned $43.25 in sales. Most pots sold for less than $4, although Baca did earn $25 for a single pot, and one San Ildefonso pot sold for $11.

While traders had sent materials for exhibition in past fairs, they had not been allowed to make sales. That changed in 1927, when traders placed a variety of stock for sale on consignment. Santa Fe store owner Julius Gans sold silver and stonework made by Reyes Suina and Luis Ortiz of Cochiti. Traders B. I. Staples of Coolidge, Roscoe Rice of Acoma, and Wick Miller of San Isidro also sold pieces.

As before, potters, weavers, sand painters, and jewelers gave demonstrations for fairgoers. Other Indians demonstrated grinding corn using manos and metates, and making *piki*, or paper bread. In the patio of the Palace of the Governors, Indians shot bows and arrows, threw rabbit sticks, and demonstrated other sports and games. A considerable effort was made in 1927 to include Indian schools and Pueblo day schools in the fair, with good results. Acomita, San Felipe, Santo Domingo, Laguna, and Jemez day schools, and the Santa Fe Indian School, all sent exhibits.

THE 1928 SOUTHWEST INDIAN FAIR

The 1928 fair took place on August 31 and September 1, corresponding with Santa Fe Fiesta. Chapman noted that the fiesta that year was a "little Fiesta, of, by, and for Santa Fe . . . a little homemade affair" (Hodge Papers). It featured no Indian ceremonials or dramas.

The event was small for several reasons. First, La Fonda Hotel was being remodeled that year, which limited accommodations for Santa Fe visitors. Second, the Albuquerque Chamber of Commerce hosted the First American Pageant in 1928, with financial backing of almost $30,000: "three times our Fiesta expenditure in its most expensive form," noted Kenneth Chapman (Hodge Papers). The Albuquerque pageant was a four-day event with parades, concerts, dances, arts and crafts, races, and night dramas performed before a papier-mâché pueblo. It was intended to stimulate tourism.

Even with this competition, the 1928 Indian Fair did as well as in previous years, recording gifts of $498, gate receipts of $252, and sales of $932. The prize list published for the "Seventh Annual Southwest Indian Fair" included fifty-three categories. Dropped from the list were prizes for blankets (primarily Navajo), while the number of beadwork and painting prize classifications was reduced. Included were six categories exclusively for school exhibits. The rules remained exactly the same as in previous years, and an announcement at the bottom of the list read, "The admission to the Fair is free to Indians wearing something characteristically Indian."

Pottery prize winners were consistent with those of prior years: Tonita Roybal won first place and Maria Martinez won second place at San Ildefonso. Martinez also won a special award of $10 for being the best-dressed Pueblo woman at the fair. Lufina Baca again won for the best undecorated pot over fifty inches in circumference. No Nambe or Tesuque potters won awards. Newcomers Manuelita Cruz and Petrusina Naranjo, from Ohkay Owingeh and Santa Clara, respectively, also won pottery awards.

89KCO.24.2
Chapman's list

1929

660 East Garcia Street
Santa Fe, N. M.

Prize list — San Juan

CK 165. J. B. Ortiz 1st prize Willow baskets. class 2. 4. –
" 169. Flora Archuleta 2nd   Emb. dress. class. 8. 5. –
" 171. Gregorita Cruz 2nd   dance kilt " 9 3. –
" 188. José Maria Cata 1st   beadwork " 18 5. –
" 190. Mrs. Jo Montoya 1st   " 20 5. –
" 196. Encarnacion Montoya Men's Costume " 24 10. –
200. Senaida Cruz. 2nd prize Ceremonial object 34. 3. –
202. Ventura Montoya Special women's boots 36. 5. –

40. –

Agricultural prizes — class 36 special.

K. 209. Fabian Cata. 1st prize White corn. 2. —
210. José A. Montoya 2nd   1. —
212. Alcario Archuleta 2nd   New Wheat 1. — 2. —
213. Crucito Cata 2nd   Oats 1. 2. —
214. Dora Cata 1st   green string beans.
   Basket of vegetables 2. 4. —
215. Dora Archuleta 1st   groups pumpkins 2. 1. —
216. Max Cruz. 2nd   Basket of vegetables
   1st   Carrots - 2. –
   2nd   Tomatoes 1. —
217. Juan Jabaldon 1st   Green chili 1. — 4. —
218. Antonio Oyngue 2nd   Squash 2. —
219. Ventura Montoya 1st   Squash 1. —
   1st   Indian Cookery 2. — 4. —
220. Maria Catencio 2nd   Brown corn 1. —
221. Filaberto Cata 1st   Brown corn 1. —
222. José B. Abeyta 1st   Cantaloupe 2. —
223. Santos Cruz 1st   Oats
224. Emilio Archuleta 2nd   green chili 2. 3. —
225. Avelino Cruz 1st   Indian Melons 1.
   Dried Beans 3. — 4. —

THE 1929 SOUTHWEST INDIAN FAIR

An article in *El Palacio* reported that visitors to the 1928 Santa Fe Fiesta and Indian Fair had missed the presentation of Indian ceremonials and the dramas of Indian life that year. The article went on to suggest that the Gallup Inter-Tribal Indian Ceremonial (founded in 1922) might take the place of Santa Fe Fiesta in this regard.

This statement, probably written by Hewett loyalist Paul Walter, apparently incited the Indian Fair Committee to put on the most successful fair to date in 1929, with total earnings of $4,447 for the three-day event. With every reason to be proud, the committee published a small brochure after the 1929 fair, reporting on the earnings and the amount returned to the pueblos, along with the following message:

> The results of the Fair are already evident. In several of the Pueblos the pottery has so improved that it has become the chief source of income to the village. The interest of the Indian women is so keen that they can name the prize winners for years back.

The brochure also highlighted the fair's success with Pueblo schoolchildren: "In accepting from the schools only such exhibits as conform to the policy of the Fair, the production of genuine Indian art has been encouraged among the school children."

Again, pottery prize winners and high sellers were consistent with those from previous years. Pottery sales totaled 568 pieces. Maria Martinez earned $176.25. Tonita Roybal took home $93.15, and Lufina Baca earned $28. In addition, new prize categories were added for vegetables, including Indian white corn, tobacco, wheat, beans, tomatoes, pumpkins, and squash. The prizes all went to Ohkay Owingeh people.

THE 1930 SOUTHWEST INDIAN FAIR

The 1930 Indian Fair demonstrated an assurance buoyed, no doubt, by the success of the previous year. The rules were substantially revised for the first time in the fair's history. For instance, the fair was now willing to accept "modifications from traditional shapes and designs . . . if by the changes the articles become more suitable for the white man's uses and . . . thus more saleable." Such modified pieces, however, were segregated and marked "adaptations"; a prize was offered for the best of the same. On August 31, the *New Mexican* reported that the fair "offers almost the only opportunity [for artists] to compare their work with that of others, and furnishes the element of rivalry among the craftsmen and women."

The prize list was expanded to include seventy-eight categories, including new awards for agricultural exhibits, block prints, dolls, and blankets. Pottery continued to be judged under three classes: (1) best piece from each pueblo or tribe; (2) best undecorated jar over fifty inches in circumference from the entire field; and (3) best decorated jar over fifty inches in circumference from the entire field.

Total receipts were $5,378, which included gifts of $1,410, a gate of $731, and $74 from the Fiesta Council to pay for the transportation of Indian dancers. Indian artists earned $580 in prize money and $2,397 in sales. Maria Martinez ($152), Tonita Roybal ($90.50), and Lufina Baca ($28) continued their dominance of the pottery market. However, Martinez's $152 probably

LUFINA BACA (SANTA CLARA) WAS THE MOST RENOWNED SANTA CLARA POTTER OF THE PERIOD, WINNING EVERY YEAR FROM 1922 TO 1931.

included sales of pots made by her sisters Desideria and Anna, whose names do not appear in the records from 1930.

New names in the sales records for the 1930 fair included Rose Gonzales, Ramona Gonzales, Van Gutierrez, and Tomasita Montoya. These names indicate that a new generation of potters was emerging. Born in the twentieth century, these potters were more willing to have their names either written on pots or associated with them. In addition, as pottery increasingly became made solely for sale, Pueblo women by necessity became less shy in their dealings with the non-Pueblo world.

CHANGES: THE 1931 INDIAN FAIR

The tenth annual Indian Fair was different from those of previous years. Rather than indoors, it was held under the portal of the Palace of the Governors, and exhibitors sold directly to customers. A copy of a June 6, 1931, letter sent to Pueblo governors, signed by fair committee member Margaret McKittrick Burge, reveals much about the 1931 fair:

> The Indian Fair at the Santa Fe Fiesta is going to be different this year. It will be September 7 and 8....
>
> Before the Fair we are going to buy the best pottery, drums, bead work, etc., that we can find. We will buy all these things before the time of the Fair. All of these things will be put together as an exhibit, but none of it will be for sale. We will not sell any of it because we will send it to New York. Next winter in New York there will be an exhibition of Indian Art from all over the United States. So we will send the exhibit from here to New York so that the New Mexico Indians will have their part in the exhibit in New York. All the pottery, drums, embroidery, weaving, and bead work for this exhibit, we will buy before the time of the Fair, and we will not sell any of it in Santa Fe because we want to send it to the big exposition in New York, so that the people in New York will know what beautiful things are made in New Mexico.

A rainstorm had washed out the 1930 Indian encampment. In addition, the feeding of dancers and crafts demonstrators had cost the Indian Fair Committee about $400 in 1929 and 1930. Burge's letter goes on to make it clear that the committee would no longer be responsible for such expenses or for the welfare of Indian people coming to Santa Fe:

We would like to have the Indians make their own camp this year. We will have a nice place for the Indians by themselves, but they must bring their own tents and their own things to eat, because we will not have any kitchen this year.... The Indians must come to Santa Fe in their own cars or wagons this year, and bring hay for their own horses.

The committee would not sponsor any dances in 1931 either. Nevertheless, Burge's letter did encourage Pueblo people to come to the fair prepared to dance:

In the dancing, we will have a place where the Indians can dance, and we will have places where people can sit and watch. We will take tickets at the gate and the money that people pay at the door will be divided among all the Indians that dance, but we will not pay anybody to come in and dance. They must come in and dance, and if they put on good dances people will pay a lot of money to come and see them. We will not charge anything for helping the Indians put [on] their dances like this.

Asking people to organize their own transportation, camping, and dance performances was an acknowledgement from the Indian Fair Committee that Pueblo people could take care of themselves. The paternalistic tone of Edgar L. Hewett's Indian Fair was diminishing. However, the surviving expense records show that the committee did pay for girls' dance costumes, as well as small amounts for firewood and tent hauling.

The most profound change in 1931 was that committee members would not sell for the artists. Rather, Indian people were expected to sell their own works:

If the Indians wish to sell their things at the Fair, we will have some place where they can sell their things, but we cannot sell their things for them. Each person must sell their things, each one for himself, and we will have a place for the Indians to do this.

The letter concluded:

If any of your people want to come in, will you please let us know before the fourth of July, so that we will know how much room there must be for the people. Please let us hear from you before the fourth of July how many of your people will come to Santa Fe for the Fair because we want to have enough room for everybody.

The changes might have stemmed from financial concerns or simply from the realization that the fair had fulfilled its original purpose: to encourage and revive Indian arts and to establish markets for these arts. By the 1930s, Indian artistic revivals in general were becoming more Indian-centered and less about what Anglos wanted. Moris Burge, a fieldworker with the National Association on Indian Affairs, explained, "This stimulus to Indian culture could have important results in maintaining tribal self-respect and raising it to a high level . . . it could increase tribal coherence, and engender in crafts-men a pride in the past achievement of their people" (Burge 1935:1).

The revamped 1931 fair was another success. The list of prize categories was exactly the same as the previous year's. However, the list was typed and mimeographed instead of being commercially printed—perhaps to save money. In the pottery category, Crucita Trujillo of Ohkay Owingeh won a special award for a "new style of pottery"—an incised style developed by a group of eight Ohkay Owingeh potters. Organizers also gave awards for the best dance performance and the best Pueblo costume.

As Burge had explained in her letter, a significant amount of artwork had been purchased ahead of time for inclusion in an upcoming exhibition in New York, the Exposition of Indian Tribal Arts. All the prizewinning work would be for sale as part of the museum exhibition.

PUEBLO CRAFTSMEN, PALACE OF THE GOVERNORS, 1937. PABLITA VELARDE (SANTA CLARA), GOUACHE ON PAPER.

CHAPTER 7

TRANSITION: 1932 TO 1940

THE 1931 INDIAN FAIR was the last one to follow the format established in 1922. In 1932 the fair was instead taken to the pueblos and the day schools, primarily during feast days (religious ceremonies to honor pueblos' patron saints). In addition, the Indian Fair Committee worked with trader-established fairs at Zuni, Gallup, and Shiprock.

The changes occurred because Indian Fair organizers worried that not enough Indian people were able to see the prizewinners. "Consequently in 1932 it was decided to discontinue the annual fair in Santa Fe and to send judges and award prizes at fairs held by the Indians in their respective pueblos, or, in the case of reservations, at the agencies," explained Margaret McKittrick Burge (1935:2).

In 1932 Indian Fair Committee members served as judges at individual fairs at Ohkay Owingeh, Cochiti, Picuris, Acoma, Shiprock, and Zia, and at the Santa Fe Indian School. The Ohkay Owingeh, Picuris, and Acoma fairs were staged on the day of their traditional patron saint observances. These fairs were little more than a room at the pueblo day school, where women brought their pottery for judging. Substantially less was spent on prize money, and no costs were incurred for setting up the events

At Ohkay Owingeh, teacher's aide Regina Cata requested that Kenneth Chapman come to help with the school's fair, to be held on June 24. He and others traveled to Ohkay Owingeh but spent only an hour there. The winners at Ohkay Owingeh—Romancita Archuleta, Gregorita Trujillo, Crucita Trujillo, Juana Garcia, and John Trujillo—were the same people who had been winning in Santa Fe. At Picuris, the committee encouraged the development of clay casserole dishes. "We are making frequent visits to the pueblo and hope to establish a productive industry there," the committee noted.

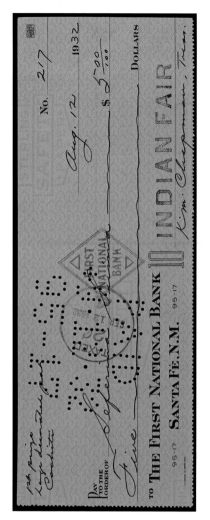

A CANCELED AND CASHED
CHECK FOR HERRERA'S FIRST-
PLACE PRIZE, 1932. PHOTO BY
BLAIR CLARK.

ESTEFANITA (OR STEPHANITA)
HERRERA OF COCHITI HOLDS
HER AWARD-WINNING BOWL,
JULY 14, 1932. FROM 1932 TO
1935, INDIAN FAIR COMMITTEE
MEMBERS TRAVELED TO THE
PUEBLOS TO JUDGE POTTERY
RATHER THAN HOLDING A FAIR
IN SANTA FE.

In 1933 committee members served as judges at the Zuni and Shiprock fairs, the Gallup Inter-Tribal Ceremonial, and fairs at San Ildefonso, Cochiti, and Ohkay Owingeh. The committee gave out its own awards at these fairs. Local Indian agencies, traders, and other supporters gave additional prizes.

The committee found that outside of Santa Fe, quality was lower and so were judging standards. At the local fairs, inexpensively made pieces were displayed alongside those that were well made and that featured culturally based materials, techniques, and designs. The Shiprock fair had no standards for judging, no published prize list, and no qualified judges. Awards were offered only for blankets, silver, and paintings. Exhibitors displayed wares such as bordered, commercially dyed floor rugs developed by traders for curio-buying tourists. In 1933 Indian Fair Committee judges reported that the Shiprock fair was "the most disappointing, even worse than that of 1932."

By this time, Pueblo potters had become more and more dependent on financial income derived from the arts. And as always, larger, more expensive pieces were harder to sell than quickly made and cheap souvenirs. As a result, potters never stopped producing small pieces that could be purchased by tourists for ten or twenty-five cents as mementos of their visits to the Southwest. The difference now was that many of these small pieces were black-on-black and polished blackwares.

The combination of potters' need for money, the rapidly growing fame of black-on-black pottery, and the growing demand from tourists had exactly the opposite effect the fair organizers desired: they were seeing an extraordinary amount of replication rather than innovation by potters. Such trends were what Indian Fair organizers had always desired to combat. NMAIA secretary Maria Chabot would later recall, "We all deplored this because it wasn't Indian art."

INDIAN FAIR JUDGES EXAM, 1932. KENNETH CHAPMAN DEVELOPED GUIDELINES AND A TEST TO HELP QUALIFY JUDGES TO BETTER EVALUATE ARTWORK. PHOTO BY BLAIR CLARK.

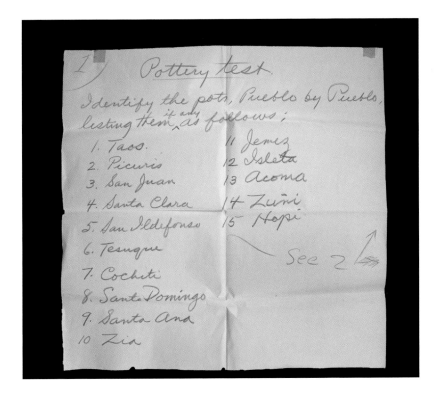

SANTO DOMINGO POTTERY SELL-
ERS BY THE HIGHWAY, C. 1940.
PHOTOGRAPH BY T. HARMON
PARKHURST.

To a great extent, the work of the Indian Fair Committee overlapped with that of the New Mexico Association on Indian Affairs. Most of the memberships were also shared. NMAIA had been established in 1922 as a political advocacy group to support Native land and water rights and other governance and health issues. To eliminate duplicated efforts, in May 1934 the committee dissolved itself, turned over $419 to the NMAIA Arts and Crafts Committee, and officially became part of that organization.

The new committee drafted a new set of rules and prize lists for use at pueblo-based fairs. The rules, classifications, and prize amounts were the same as those used at the Santa Fe fairs. In 1934 fairs were held at Ohkay Owingeh, Tesuque, Picuris, Nambe, and Cochiti; school fairs were held at Taos, Tesuque, and Ohkay Owingeh; and agency-sponsored fairs were held at Zuni, San Carlos, and Gallup. Margaret McKittrick Burge (1935:2–3) reported on the year's work:

> At Tesuque not one souvenir "rain-god" was present, and there were some 15 pieces of traditional types, all of good quality. There were one or two developments in the way of cookie jars made from a red cooking clay which were attractive, useful, and of a simple primitive shape. Katherine Vigil exhibited a jar of highly polished brown ware which received a prize for modern development. The Nambe Fair was the first ever held at that Pueblo. Most of the work was rough and crude, but it was commendable that this small and impoverished community should make such an effort. Particularly interesting was some handspun cotton. At Picuris the pottery was displayed in the new Community House, each potter having her work on a separate table. The work was of good quality although there remains much to be done in finally persuading the women to produce shapes which are simple and have utility value. At San Juan several hundred jars were shown, and naturally in such a large number there was variation in quality. The first prize went to a large piece with finely incised design carried out in straight lines.

Despite the overall positive report, NMAIA commitment to the pueblo-based fairs began to waiver. Several of the fairs had been dissatisfying. As Burge reported:

> The Zuni Fair was a delightful revelation of the variety of crafts which are still practiced in that Pueblo and adjacent villages. But

the displays mutely confirmed the pessimistic reports on the pottery making in that Pueblo. It is art which is rapidly dying and unfortunately no plan has yet been suggested whereby it can again be made into a useful, living activity. The Cochiti Fair was distinctly disappointing, not one fine piece being shown, so no prizes were awarded. (Burge 1935:2–3)

Judge Kenneth Chapman echoed this assessment: We "found the Arts and Crafts exhibition [at Cochiti] so disgracefully poor that we gave reprimands instead of prizes" (Kenneth Chapman Papers).

In September and October 1935, the NMAIA discussed whether it should continue the local fairs, which were draining the staff and financial resources of the association. Members considered ending the commitment to the indi-

THE INDIAN FAIR
PUEBLO: *Cochiti*
MADE BY: *Crepecia Quintana*
PRICE:

vidual fairs and reinstating fairs in Santa Fe. NMAIA secretary Maria Chabot remembered in an interview many years later that the idea was to again give "strangers in our midst [tourists] an opportunity to see what experts consider good Indian art and workmanship."

Maria Chabot proposed holding the fairs on Saturdays in summer under the portal of the Palace of the Governors. At the June 11, 1936, NMAIA meeting, she told the membership "that the market plan had come to her after seeing the markets held in all the little villages in old Mexico on their fiesta days." The meeting minutes explained,

> Miss Chabot's plan was that all Indians be invited to come in each week but that one or two pueblos only would be featured each Saturday and these awarded prizes and provided with transportation.

THIS TAG WAS WRITTEN BY MARTHA WHITE AND ADHERED TO THE BOTTOM OF A COCHITI POT MADE BY CREPECIA (AGRAPINA) QUINTANA FOR EITHER THE 1928 OR 1929 FAIR. THE INVENTORY NUMBER ("86") AND PRICE ENABLED THE FAIR COMMITTEE TO TRACK SALES AND PAY THE EXHIBITORS. OTHER THAN AT SAN ILDEFONSO, POTTERS WERE RELUCTANT TO SIGN THE BOTTOM OF A POT, ALTHOUGH THE FAIR COMMITTEE BEGAN URGING POTTERS TO SIGN THEIR WORK BY THE MID-1920S. MRS. QUINTANA'S NAME ON THE TAG SERVED AS A DE-FACTO SIGNATURE.

After the prizes had been awarded there would be a talk explaining why the prizes had been awarded.

Chabot spent the month of June visiting individual pueblos and found a positive response to her plan. The day school teachers were particularly helpful in disseminating the word.

However, a teacher in Tesuque expressed concern that brightly painted pottery might be prohibited at the Saturday markets and that such a ruling might start a split between the village's good potters and those who made the more poorly painted type. In the end, no restrictions were placed on what could be sold in the markets, but NMAIA judges would attach small red-bordered stickers, or "labels of approval," to those pieces deemed to represent good Indian art. So although people could sell ashtrays and brightly painted wares, these pieces would not be sanctioned by the NMAIA.

Year by year during the 1920s, the Indian Fair Committee had admitted innovations to Indian Fairs, as artists mastered the construction of new objects such as ashtrays, cigarette boxes, candlesticks, animal figurines, lamp bases, and decorated tiles. The committee had recognized that the mere imitation of one's ancestral art could be stultifying. The NMAIA similarly realized, "If native art is to survive it must be a growing thing, suitable for the time and circumstance in which it is made and it must be created out of the imagination of the individual craftsman, not merely a faithful reproduction of the work of his ancestors" (Dietrich 1936).

As plans for the Saturday markets took shape, Chabot and others wrote a series of articles for *New Mexico Magazine*, published from February 1936 to July 1937. The articles carried the authoritative notation, "Published with the Approval of the Laboratory of Anthropology." Written to educate people about what constituted authentic and good Indian art, the articles examined Pueblo and Navajo painting, baskets, embroidery, dress, pottery, blankets, dances, sandpainting, jewelry, and their modern adaptations.

THE SATURDAY MARKETS

The Saturday markets began in July 1936. Under Chabot's plan, one or two pueblos were featured each Saturday. While artists from other pueblos were welcome to sell their wares, only arts and crafts from the featured villages were eligible for judging and prizes. Each pueblo or village was assigned a certain space under the portal.

The *New Mexican* reported that the first week the market featured only fifty craftspeople. But the numbers grew quickly. At first, all the artists could fit under the portal of the Palace of the Governors. But toward the latter part of the summer, the sales area expanded around the corners to Lincoln and Washington avenues.

The first featured pueblos of 1936 were San Ildefonso and Tesuque. "Practically every potter from San Ildefonso had made especially fine wares for this market," wrote Chabot in an NMAIA report. More than one thousand pieces of shining black pottery were displayed, and sales were heavy. A first-place prize went to Katherine Vigil of Tesuque for her traditional pottery. This award apparently inspired other Tesuque potters, who the following week brought similar wares to sell.

On July 18 prizes were offered to Santa Clara artists; fifteen arrived by bus and another twenty or so by private car. Chabot counted more than one hundred artists sitting under the portal that day and noted, "Santa Clara contributed at least 25 potters a week" throughout the markets.

The Nambe Women's Club was also invited. This group of eight women came in July and every Saturday afterward during 1936, bringing woven belts, embroideries, curtains, paintings, and kilts. (Most of the kilts were sold to other Indian people, probably to use in ceremonial dances.) In August Jemez basket weavers brought plaited grain-winnowing baskets, which sold readily to other Indian people as well as to tourists. The following Saturday about fifty-five Ohkay Owingeh potters and craftspeople were on hand. Chabot reported that Ohkay Owingeh averaged twenty-five vendors each week during the remainder of the summer, even when the pueblo wasn't featured.

Chabot continued her report: "August 1st a bus went to Santo Domingo, picked up 10 potters, proceeded to Cochiti and picked up 10 more.... We had possibly 20 Santo Domingo Indians under the portal with their very poor pottery—all quite indignant that they couldn't sell their wares. We believe it did them good to associate with the fine Santa Clara and San Ildefonso pottery."

The *New Mexican* reported that Santo Domingo traders also participated in the market, selling Navajo rugs and silver jewelry. Cochiti village members returned each week—twenty-five or thirty strong—selling hundreds of drums and beaded rabbit's feet. About forty potters who had never been to Santa Fe came from Acoma and Laguna one week. They viewed their visit as "more than a business trip . . . it is a schooling . . . to 'find' new designs—new old designs [at the Laboratory of Anthropology]," explained the newspaper. August 15 featured the work of about twenty Isleta potters and weavers, and August 22 featured the pueblos of Zia and Jemez. Overall, each week averaged about 150 artists at the market.

LOGISTICS

In organizing the markets, Chabot made two interesting breaks with tradition. First, she contacted the potters directly, asking them to participate instead of going through each pueblo's governor. She also asked potters to help in both publicizing and judging the markets. As Indian people had not always felt welcome in Santa Fe, Chabot and other NMAIA members employed their powers of persuasion and the promise of transportation to and from town to attract them. "They came to town when they knew they were acceptable in town," Chabot explained. She appealed to Maria Martinez and other potters personally to help spread the word and convince people to participate.

The Santa Fe Chamber of Commerce and local merchants also needed convincing. Chabot enlisted the assistance of traders James Seligman and Jim Macmillan (of the Spanish and Indian Trading Company) in publicizing the market, while the Fred Harvey Company and other traders offered no help, "probably seeing [the markets] as competition." Although the shop owners were concerned about being undersold, "the Indians seldom if ever undersold the Santa Fe Indian shops."

The citizens of Santa Fe still carried some deep-seated prejudices against Indian people. Only the gas station on the corner of Washington and Palace allowed Indians to use its toilets; Hewett's museum did not. Many of the plaza merchants also had low opinions of Indian people, even though "the money made by the Indians went right back into these stores," remarked Chabot.

The NMAIA sent buses to the pueblos to bring people to town for the day. Both the buses and the drivers were retained through negotiations with the Bureau of Indian Affairs. After the judging and the initial flurry of activity each Saturday, potters were loaded back onto buses in the late morning for a trip to the Laboratory of Anthropology to see the pottery collections. The first goal of the market was educational, and this visit was intended to remind potters of what good work should be. The NMAIA urged the potters to "stay with their past and to keep our [non-Indian] culture out of it." The women were "exulted by what they saw" and "went immediately to their area [the shelves that held their pueblo's pottery]," Chabot reported. Chabot and the rest of the NMAIA hoped these visits would stimulate interest in good pots and would encourage artists to make bigger pieces, for the "survival of pottery depended on quality."

The prizes at the Saturday markets were $2 for first place and $1 for second place. In 1936 Santa Clara artists received a total of $29 in prizes. Ohkay Owingeh artists won $16, San Ildefonso and Tesuque artists took home $6, and Nambe artists collected $3. Only objects from the week's featured pueblos were judged and awarded prizes.

Chabot had originally intended Indian people to serve as judges. She asked Maria Martinez, Tonita Peña (a Cochiti painter), and Severa Tafoya (a Santa Clara potter) to do the judging. But they were unwilling, telling Chabot they did not want to judge each other. Thus the judges were non-Indians by default. Kenneth Chapman and archaeologist Harry Mera did the job—their sixteenth year serving in this capacity.

In addition to cash, prizes included groceries donated by local merchants. The groceries were intended to be a lesson in proper nutrition for Indian people, with an emphasis on fresh fruits and vegetables. Prize ribbons for honorable mention and other honors were also given.

After the judging, Chapman was supposed to give two short talks under the portal on the objects being offered for sale. However, he could not hold the crowd's attention, and this feature of the market was quickly dropped. Instead, Chapman painted a four-by-six-foot sign telling tourists how to test for a good piece of pottery.

The last two markets of 1936 were both unscheduled. On the weekend of the Gallup Ceremonial, no market had been planned. Nonetheless, many artists came to the portal to sell. The following weekend was Santa Fe Fiesta. Indians had not officially participated in fiestas since 1931, although Indian potters and painters probably sold works on the front steps and on the Lincoln Street side of the Fine Arts Museum during those years. But now, in 1936, the Fiesta Council asked potters to sell under the portal during the three-day event. Sales were reported to be low because of visitors' interest in other attractions and because of the depletion of vendors' inventory from a successful summer of selling. The Fiesta Council awarded prizes to the artists in the form of groceries and canned fruit.

No accounting was made of sales for the entire summer, although Chabot noted that Severa Tafoya averaged $16 a week in sales, with the "lesser" potters of her village making between $4 and $6 each week. When the summer ended, Chabot took a job with the new Indian Arts and Crafts Board as a field-worker. She traveled around the United States for two years, working to establish successful arts and crafts revival programs as she had in Santa Fe.

MORE MARKETS

No Saturday markets were held in 1937, but people did sell under the portal during Santa Fe Fiesta that year. In 1938 and 1939, the NMAIA again sponsored Saturday markets, with a total of eight markets, plus a Fiesta Market, each summer. For an unexplained reason, a number of vessels over fifty inches in circumference were on sale at these markets, leading Kenneth Chapman to comment, "It was like old times." Among these were pieces made by Margaret Tafoya and Maria and Julian Martinez.

Maria Martinez remembered this about the large black-on-black piece she and her husband made that year: "I sold it to Henry Dendahl . . . and he said, 'how much, Maria?' and I say, 'oh, you can give me whatever you want.' And he gave me forty. I nearly fall down. Forty dollars and three shawls." (Spivey 1979:50).

Kenneth Chapman left us this assessment of the 1938 market:

> The Portal of the Old Palace is a public thoroughfare and it is impossible to estimate [visitor] attendance. The total was well above 8,000 for the series [entire summer]. . . . Sales were made directly by the Indians, and there is no way of estimating total [cash received]. The average attendance of exhibitors and their families was about 150, and reached over 300 on Sept. 3d [fiesta]. The average number of exhibitors was about 75. The overflow often extended up the streets on either side of the Old Palace. Some exhibitors seemed to sell little or nothing. Others took in as much as $75 in a day (there were no Navajo blankets, and very few large items such as embroidered mantas or other high priced things). If sales averaged only $3.00 per week for each of the exhibitors, the total for the series would be $1,800. I believe a safe guess would be nearer $2,500. (SAR/Kenneth Chapman Papers)

THE IMPACT OF THE SATURDAY MARKETS

The Saturday markets facilitated substantial change in a short period. Previously, when Pueblo people had participated in Indian Fairs, they mostly had been silent partners—demonstrating, performing, and adding color to the

POTTERS SELL THEIR WORK AT
THE 1937 SANTA FE FIESTA. NO
OFFICIAL INDIAN FAIR WAS HELD
THAT SUMMER, BUT POTTERS
AND OTHER CRAFTSPEOPLE
SOLD UNDER THE PORTAL OF
THE PALACE OF THE GOVERNORS
MOST WEEKENDS.

scene. At the Saturday markets, artists now represented themselves, set their own prices, and sold their own wares. Instead of Pueblo men, museum staff, the Indian Fair Committee, or the NMAIA, the potters themselves (mostly female) interpreted their culture for the outside world. The markets also allowed artists from different pueblos to see each other's work. Thereafter, there was a relatively easy flow of ideas and styles between artists, alleviating

TRINIDAD MEDINA (ZIA) WON A RIBBON FOR THIS LARGE JAR AT THE 1939 INDIAN MARKET. HER GRANDSON DESCRIBED THE POT AS BIGGER THAN HIS GRAND-MOTHER.

some of the rivalries that had divided families and villages but also hardening factionalism and dissent among families and in the villages.

The ramifications went beyond Santa Fe. At the 1939 Panama-Pacific International Exposition in San Francisco, for instance, the Indian Arts and Crafts Board hosted an Indian market modeled on those held in Santa Fe. The San Francisco event was intended to illustrate the utility of Indian-made arts and crafts for the modern American home.

As Indian crafts grew more popular, non-Pueblo people began coming to villages to buy pottery directly from makers. In addition, the precedent of Indian people selling their wares under the portal was now established. Even outside of market days, potters started coming to Santa Fe to sell their wares.

CHAPTER 8

STAGNATION AND CHANGE: 1940 TO 1967

===========

WORLD WAR II brought an end to the Saturday markets, but Fiesta Markets continued as part of a smaller, more local, wartime Santa Fe Fiesta. Throughout most of the 1940s, a first-place win at Fiesta Market paid $3, and second place paid $1.50. Pieces over fifty inches in circumference could win either a $5 first- or a $3 second-place prize. In 1949 prize money was returned to the 1920s levels of $5 for first, $3 for second, and $10 for the best piece over fifty inches in circumference.

Pottery prices had changed very little over the years. Pieces generally sold for $2.50 to $4.00, with larger pieces obtaining higher prices. In 1952 Margretta Dietrich (1952:7) wrote that "fewer large storage jars appeared and the prices for the few brought to the Market increased. In the early years they had sold for as little as $15; at the 1951 Market one large black Santa Clara storage jar [made by Margaret Tafoya] sold for $75."

The number of exhibitors receiving awards was dramatically reduced after 1948, when the NMAIA stopped awarding first- and second-place prizes to each pueblo. In 1949 prizes were given for the "best articles in each class in the whole market, not to each pueblo as formerly." That year there were eight entry classes: pottery, textiles, ceremonial drums, painting, jewelry, baskets, leather goods, and woodcarving. For the first time, Hopi kachina figures, conspicuously absent since the fair's beginning, were included in the market, the woodcarving class having been created just for them. (In deference to the secrecy concerning Rio Grande kachinas, the NMAIA had kept the carved figures out of previous fairs and markets so as not to offend Rio Grande peoples.)

OHKAY OWINGEH POTTERES
AT THE 1948 FIESTA MARKET.
PHOTO BY ROBERT H. MARTIN.

DANCE PERFORMANCES

In 1944, during World War II, Cochiti and San Ildefonso people danced at Fiesta Market to raise money to help the NMAIA send more than 105 Christmas gift boxes to Pueblo soldiers overseas. After that, Pueblo dances became a permanent part of Fiesta Market. In 1945 the association earned $700 from the dances, twice what it had earned the previous year. Thereafter, the NMAIA sponsored Fiesta Market dance performances as its primary means of raising funds. After 1948 interest in Fiesta Market dance performances dropped, however. As a result, NMAIA revenues also dwindled.

ONGOING TROUBLES

Throughout the 1950s, Fiesta Market participants were plagued by the same problems they had experienced at previous fairs and markets. Sallie Wagner, a 1950s-era Fiesta Market organizer, remembered that plaza merchants still resented artists "cluttering up the front of their stores." Most toilet facilities were still off-limits to Indians. La Fonda charged five cents to use its toilets; the Museum of New Mexico's Hall of Ethnology was guarded; and the palace and the Fine Arts Museum were closed on fiesta days.

Under the portal, chaos reigned for the artists. There were no space assignments as there had been during Saturday markets; establishing your space was a free-for-all. People showed up at 3:30 a.m. to claim a good spot and held onto it throughout the fiesta by sleeping on the sidewalk. According to NMAIA meeting minutes, in 1949 the Women's Club Library Association complained "relative to Indians sleeping in the backyard of the Library. It was claimed that they caused damage to the upkeep of the property and had left all kinds of dirt and trash in the yard." As a remedy, the NMAIA urged (to no avail) that the city provide "some type of accommodations with necessary toilet facilities for future fiestas."

Fiesta Market participation leveled off at about 125 artists, or about 300 Indian people if you counted the artists' families. They filled the portal along the front of the palace. Some sat on the curb, with the remainder spilling down the east and west sides of the building. In 1956 the Museum of New Mexico's board of regents gave the NMAIA permission to provide shade for these individuals with a framework of pipes covered by tarpaulins. But according to board meeting minutes, "The City Manager . . . acting under the instructions from the Chairman of Police . . . had refused permission to erect the awnings."

CHANGE: 1958

The 1958 Fiesta Market brought some big changes to the proceedings. That year, individual spaces were assigned for the first time. Each space was forty-two by forty-eight inches and was designated by chalk lines drawn on the ground. Each artist got a different space assignment each day. In a Fiesta Committee notice, participants were told, "Do Not sit down until the officers tell you where to sit, because you will not have the same place each day. See chart on the front door of the Museum."

The assignments meant that artists no longer needed to sleep under the portal to hold their spaces. "All the pueblos were enthusiastic in their endorse-

FAMILIES SLEPT UNDER THE PORTAL IN THE 1950S TO HOLD SPOTS FOR SELLING THEIR WORK AT FIESTA MARKET.

ment of the plan—all but Santo Domingo, which heretofore has appropriated and held onto the greater part of the portal, spreading their stuff out for as much as six or seven feet," noted NMAIA meeting minutes. Also in 1958, a campground, complete with bathrooms, was provided for Indian participants at Fort Marcy. These were the first accommodations offered to people since 1930. Judging took place on Saturday morning, with judges "racing along booth to booth, trying not to miss anything or not see something before it was sold," according to museum curator and archaeologist Marge Lambert, who served as a market organizer and judge in the 1950s. By then, prize money for large pots and water jars had increased to $12.50 for first place and $7.50 for second place. In most other categories, first place earned a $7.50 prize. An Indian Arts Fund prize of $25 for the "best traditional display of work" was awarded to Lucy Lewis of Acoma that year, after two years without a worthy recipient of the award.

1953 FIESTA MARKET. PHOTOGRAPH BY T. HARMON PARKHURST.

Lambert also recalled that as people were still "buying souvenirs" and "not appreciating the artwork," judges were expected to give impromptu talks on quality in Indian art to prospective customers. That is, the association still felt the need to make sales pitches for the Indians. The Indians themselves made no sales pitches, often allowing tourists to pass by without buying anything more than cheap souvenirs.

Following the 1958 market, another change was proposed. Artists were asked to fill out applications to participate in the market. The system was designed to cut down on people selling spurious materials, such as pottery not made by family members, non-Indian-made jewelry, and objects made before the prior year's market. Applicants had to ask for space on whatever days they desired. The application also included "a statement that the applicant agrees to display for sale only articles actually handmade by himself or a member of his immediate family . . . a committee from the All-Pueblo Council will serve as watchdogs and exclude any junk" (SWAIA 1958).

MORE CHANGES

By the late 1950s, the women who had originally made the NMAIA into a powerful organization were now elderly or dead. In failing health, Margretta Dietrich resigned in 1953 after a fourteen-year tenure as president and after thirty years of leadership with the association. As the old guard fell away, the new NMAIA members, directors, and officers were less interested in the organization's political goals. Many of them were art collectors and scholars who made their livings by studying Indian culture or by selling Indian arts and crafts. Santa Fe was turning into an arts community, and the composition of the NMAIA began to reflect this change.

For their part, Indian arts and crafts makers now almost exclusively made work to sell to non-Native people. Increasingly, the NMAIA removed itself as the middleman between maker and buyer, trusting that exhibitors now knew the non-Pueblo world sufficiently to handle their own transactions.

In the fall of 1959, the NMAIA board discussed the future of the association. It considered disbanding and entertained a proposal that its work be taken over by other organizations: "For example, the Indian Arts Fund might take over . . . the Fiesta Market Committee's work." The board sent a letter to members, calling for dissolution of the organization unless people stepped forward before January 1960. A few new people joined, and the organization continued, "because it was the path of less resistance."

In the midst of the turmoil over its future, the organization changed its name from the New Mexico Association of Indian Affairs to the Southwestern Association on Indian Affairs (SWAIA). More than just an attempt to "indicate more accurately the territory we cover," reported the SWAIA newsletter in 1959, the name change symbolized a break with the past.

INNOVATIONS: 1959–1964

In 1959 Fiesta Market grew more formalized. Artist space assignments were rotated over five days, so that everyone had a chance for the best placement— by the front doors to the Palace of the Governors. SWAIA sent printed materials to prior prizewinners, including "notices, rules and regulations, prize lists, and so forth." The 1959 judging categories no longer included baskets, long a staple of the market. The jewelry category was divided into silver, turquoise, and *heshi*. A new category was added for creative new design.

In 1960 space assignments changed again. That year, SWAIA assigned spaces by pueblo instead of by individual. The Fiesta Committee also encouraged artists to "bring a small box or table to lay your things on, so people can see them without having to get down on their knees." The 1960 prize list remained the same as the year before, except that baskets were put back on the list and a miscellaneous class was removed. Another important addition was the "Maria of San Ildefonso special pottery prize for the best in Pueblo pottery," sponsored by Maria Martinez's son Popovi Da. With this prize, named for one of the pioneering artists of Indian Fair, the market had come full circle.

Since 1936, artists had been allowed to sell whatever they brought to the market, even though it might not be approved by fair organizers. In a stunning reversal, the 1960 rules stated, "Articles which are not up to the standards set by the judges will not be allowed to be displayed or sold at the Fiesta Market." To discourage Tesuque potters who painted their pieces with commercial and poster paints after they were fired, rule 3 became more specific. It read:

> Pottery must be of the type and kind which has been recognized
> by the judges in past years as measuring up to the best traditions of
> Indian pottery making. Only pottery with paint applied *before* firing
> will be considered by the judges.

ROSE GONZALES (SAN ILDE-
FONSO) DISPLAYS HER POTTERY
AT A CIRCA 1955 INDIAN MARKET.

By now, potters routinely signed their own work. Increasingly, they represented themselves rather than their villages at Fiesta Market. For its part, SWAIA directly asked individual artists to participate rather than asking entire villages. By this time also, buyers were looking for specific artists' work. And when buyers purchased prizewinning pieces, they often wanted the ribbons that went with them. SWAIA was not willing to produce duplicate ribbons at this time (it began doing so in the mid-1970s), but it did provide buyers with artist certificates. SWAIA explained this to the artists: "You are entitled to keep your prize ribbons. If the one who buys your work insists on having a ribbon, ask him to see the judges."

FINALLY, INDIAN MARKET

Overshadowed by mariachi music and the Mexican flavor of Santa Fe Fiesta, in 1962 Indian Market finally moved to its own August weekend. After the split, however, some Indian artists continued to set up under the portal during fiestas for several more years, taking advantage of the crowds to sell their work.

Meanwhile, the Fiesta Council did not like the separation. Indian dances had been an interesting component of fiestas (as well as a source of revenue), and the dances did continue at fiestas for a few more years under sponsorship of the All-Indian Pueblo Council. But the dances were also the principal fund-raiser for SWAIA, and it didn't want to share this money with the Fiesta Council.

In 1962, without Santa Fe Fiesta as a backdrop, Indian Market needed to develop more excitement and a festival character. SWAIA hoped that Indian costumes would do the trick, so it instituted "the awarding of prizes to craftsmen wearing traditional Indian costumes." (This "innovation" was in fact a return to practices of the late 1920s, when Maria Martinez had repeatedly won the $10 award for best traditional costume.) SWAIA also believed that traditional clothing worn by artists would help reinforce the authentic nature of the arts being offered for sale.

INDIAN MARKET 1966. ROWS OF BOOTHS WERE ADDED ON PALACE AVENUE TO ACCOMMODATE THE RAPID INCREASE IN THE NUMBERS OF ARTISTS.

Indian Market soon spread from the portal onto the plaza. SWAIA member Rex Arrowsmith explained that in 1964 a row of booths was "erected along the entire length of the curb on the Plaza side of the street [Palace Avenue]. This structure was made of rough poles, set 8" apart, and covered with canvas awnings in brilliant gold, red and turquoise." Although the market was about the same size as in previous years—with 125 artists—"this innovation added greatly to the comfort and convenience of both craftsmen and visitors."

In 1965 SWAIA members Al Packard and Arrowsmith built two rows of twenty-five booths each in the center and along the south curb of Palace Avenue. "The Market was larger, more colorful, and more successful this year than ever before, due in part, to the additional gaily covered booths for crafts displays," wrote SWAIA in a 1965 quarterly publication. The booths—"cedar poles held up with cinder blocks"—were well-known for blowing over during August rainstorms.

In 1966 twenty-five more booths were added, providing space for seventy-five artists on Palace Avenue, in addition to the roughly one hundred under the portal. About half the booths had tables and chairs. Buyers looking for a specific artist could find him or her in an assigned booth. SWAIA (1968:3–4) boasted:

> Dozens of trading posts and curio stores offer authentic Indian-made goods, but Santa Fe's Indian Market has one distinction. Indians themselves journey to the old capital each year, bringing for display the best products of their own handwork. Thus, prospective buyers may meet and talk with the actual artist or craftsman when considering purchase of a particular item.

ART, NOT POLITICS

The NMAIA had been a political association. It had cared about the arts as a vehicle for economic change and, ultimately, financial independence for Pueblo people. The NMAIA *Newsletter* had kept members informed of pending legislation of interest to Native people and other political issues. SWAIA, by contrast, was an arts organization. Its *Quarterly of the Southwestern Association on Indian Affairs* included articles on Indian life and arts, both past and present. SWAIA members believed in the universal appeal of Indian art. Its board members were interested in the arts as a way of preserving the past rather than as a means of fostering political action.

The Quarterly of the
SOUTHWESTERN ASSOCIATION
ON INDIAN AFFAIRS, INC.

50 CENTS

Whereas early Indian fairs and markets had been concerned with the dignity and economic sovereignty of Indian people, under SWAIA, the new Indian Markets were art markets, designed for producing and selling art. In a 1960s newsletter, SWAIA promoted Indian Market as delivering "the best in the fine traditional craftsmanship for which the Indian American is famous and has received worldwide recognition." With that description front and center, Indian Market headed into the modern world.

SOUTHWESTERN INDIAN
AFFAIRS QUARTERLY, 1967

MARGARET TAFOYA (SANTA CLARA) DISPLAYS HER AWARD-WINNING POTTERY AT THE 1971 INDIAN MARKET. SHE WON BEST OF SHOW IN 1978 AND 1979. HER DAUGHTER AND GRANDDAUGHTER HAVE ALSO WON BEST OF SHOW.

CHAPTER 9

TODAY'S INDIAN MARKET:
A REMARKABLE PHENOMENON

EACH AUGUST, tens of thousands of people make their annual pilgrimage to Santa Fe's Indian Market. SWAIA sponsors the annual event, selects and vets the twelve hundred participating artists, judges work, and awards prize money of $100,000 across more than three hundred categories. It takes a year to plan and build Indian Market. For the two days of sales, fourteen square city blocks are transformed into a nirvana of Native arts.

Santa Fe gears up ahead of Indian Market with antique Indian art shows and auctions, gallery and museum openings, and 100 percent bookings at hotels. Indian Market Week, a festival of Native cultures, serves as a prelude to the two days of sales. SWAIA sometimes partners with other cultural organizations to produce a film festival, musical events, publications, and educational programming, all focused on fostering a deeper understanding and appreciation of Native cultures.

Indian Market attracts buyers and artists for unarguably the most important Indian art event in the United States. Artists spend months preparing, producing their best pieces to enter in the judging and to sell. Every art form imaginable is now eligible for entry. Some buyers plan their year around the market, making hotel reservations a year or more in advance. Others have second homes that are used sparingly, except during the Santa Fe summer. The market is the biggest cultural and economic event of the year in Santa Fe and takes over the entire downtown. The plaza area is closed to all traffic; streets are lined with 650 artists' booths, food stands, information tables, T-shirt and book sales tents, and portable toilets. The Native art world—artists, curators, and collectors—also gathers in Santa Fe for a multitude of meetings, conferences, and gallery and museum openings. Just outside the traffic barriers and banners that denote the official borders of Indian Market, hundreds of vendors sell their own Indian art in organized shows or simply by

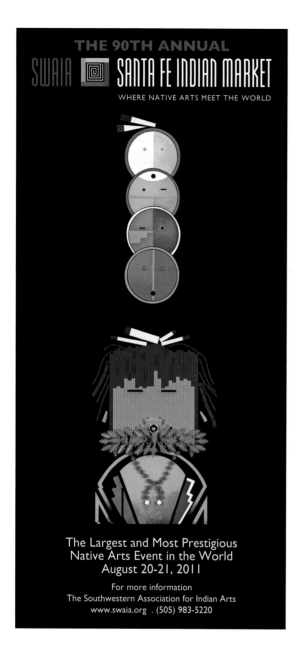

A HANDBILL ADVERTISES THE 2011 INDIAN MARKET.

placing wares on a blanket or against a low wall. Other vendors sell non-Indian ethnic clothing and baubles.

Indian Market is synonymous with authentic, handmade Indian art. The market is juried to ensure authenticity. Buyers covet tradition and come to the market to purchase directly from artists, often quizzing them about techniques and materials and, like ethnographers, often discussing their lineage and relations. Today's Indian Market is about quality—the very best artists are included, regardless of art form or whether the art is tied to a specific tribal style. Hitching Native-made art to history and tribes can be useful, but Indian Market proves again and again that it can also be stultifying.

The community of artists is eclectic, but it is a family drawn together through the commonalities of making art for non-Indians; participating in Indian Market; and honoring tribal and Native history, identity, and survival in the twenty-first century. Indian Market is steeped in tradition. Artists often say, "Our family has been participating in the market for generations."

Indian Market artists come to Santa Fe from throughout the United States and Canada, but southwestern Indian people and Pueblo people make up the overwhelming majority. Although the emphasis is on the traditional arts of jewelry, pottery, and textiles, people also display painting and sculpture incorporating many styles and techniques.

Artists covet Indian Market prizes, but it is not the prize money per se that artists desire; the money represents but a fraction of the value of an award-winning piece. Rather, receiving an Indian Market award can permanently cement an artist's reputation. Winning a high award virtually assures an artist long-term financial success, because many buyers collect art based on Indian Market awards.

The market welcomes everyone. For two days, ethnic and economic distinctions dissipate. Artists, customers, art lovers, family, and friends all become Indian Market participants. It is a grand family reunion.

Although the art and artists are the foundations of Indian Market, the buyers are just as important. These market-goers support the artists and tribal cultures through their attendance, educate themselves about Indian art and culture, befriend the artists and their families, and become vocal proponents and advocates of Indian cultures. The alliance of non-Indians and Indians at Indian Market is very much dependent on the considerable narrative power of Native arts.

There would be no Indian Market without the customers and the estimated $18 million they spend on art. These customers put another $122 million into the Santa Fe and New Mexico economies through spending at hotels, restaurants, and other businesses. Some buyers spend just a few dollars on corn necklaces. Collectors might spend tens of thousands of dollars. Some collectors have been attending Indian Market for two or three decades; they come today not only to add to their collections but also to visit with artist friends. The most devoted buyers begin arriving the evening before. Often if you are not at a prizewinning artist's booth early in the morning on opening day, there is little chance that you will be successful in purchasing the piece. Collectors and devotees sit in artists' booths or on the sidewalks, waiting for artists to arrive at 7:00 a.m. to have first crack at purchasing prizewinning pieces.

PHENOMENAL GROWTH

In 1970 Indian Market was held under the portal of the Palace of the Governors and along the north and east sides of the plaza. All two hundred artists who showed up on Saturday morning that year were given booths. The following year, a row of booths was added on the east side of the plaza, and in 1972 twenty-five more booths were added. By 1974 booths ringed the entire plaza, accommodating about five hundred artists. By 1980 the market had grown to 330 booths in rows of three on all four sides of the plaza. Fifty-nine new booths were added along Lincoln Avenue in 1982. Fifty

MARIANNE KAPOUN, KENT MCMANIS, AND JOAN CABALLERO JUDGE POTTERY AT THE 1994 INDIAN MARKET.

GIT-HOAN TSIMSHIAN DANCERS PERFORM AT THE 2010 INDIAN MARKET.

VANESSA PAUKEIGOPE JENNINGS (KIOWA) POSES WITH HER BEST OF BEADWORK AWARD WINNER, 2010.

more booths were added to Washington Avenue in 1991. By 1992 the market featured 537 booths and 1,043 artists, with 300 more artists on a waiting list.

To accommodate more artists, from 1990 to 1995, SWAIA set up forty-seven booths in the De Vargas Center, a shopping mall less than two miles from the plaza. A shuttle bus ran between the plaza and the mall. Buyers quickly caught on that SWAIA was placing second-tier artists in De Vargas, however. Most of those placed there were new to the market; many were from nonsouthwestern tribes. While nearly one hundred thousand people visited the booths on the plaza each year, only eight thousand walked by the booths at the mall. A few artists dropped out or threatened to drop out if they were assigned to De Vargas.

Originally, SWAIA built and installed artists' booths and stored them when Indian Market was over. The booths were made of cedar poles, with bases of three-pound cans filled with concrete, with colored canvas coverings on top. These booths were unstable and commonly blew down in the wind. In 1976 SWAIA designed better booths made of two-by-fours and canvas. These were more stable and provided better shelter from the weather. In 1996 SWAIA hired a contractor to install commercially made booths, some ten by ten feet and some ten by five feet. The new all-white booths were larger than the old ones, with no colored canvas tops to distract from the colors of the artwork.

By the 2012 Indian Market, 650 booths ringed the entire plaza and spread out down San Francisco Street to the St. Francis Cathedral, along Palace Avenue to Grant Avenue, down Old Santa Fe Trail to Water Street, and north on Lincoln Avenue to Federal Place—a total of fourteen square city blocks. Since collectors expect to find certain artists in certain spots year after

INDIAN MARKET 1971.

year, artists covet their booths and will do almost anything to retain them. Those artists and families who have been at the market for many decades tend to be located in the most coveted spots near the plaza.

INDIAN MARKET EVENTS

Shopping for art is just one aspect of Indian Market. Shoppers naturally get hungry, and food booths are set up on Marcy Street, along with a large covered area for resting, relaxing, and refueling. The plaza still holds some artist booths, but SWAIA sets aside most of the plaza for information booths, souvenir sales, demonstration booths, and the plaza performance stage, with seating for three hundred.

SWAIA has added several new events to Indian Market through the years. In 1990 it began a powwow, renting space from Pojoaque Pueblo and advertising the event as Spring Indian Market. The powwow generated much discussion about SWAIA's mission, however. Powwows originated with Plains Indian people, although many southwestern Native people dance at powwows. Nonetheless, some Pueblo people viewed the powwow as intrusive

FOOD BOOTH AT 2011 INDIAN MARKET

and nontraditional. Each year attendance fell and costs mounted. The last SWAIA powwow was held in 1995.

In 1995 SWAIA initiated a Masters Market. It was a separate spring market for the top thirty-five artists, rising eventually to three hundred exhibitors. But artists chosen as "masters"—those whose work sold well, senior artists, and award winners—were asked to give up their coveted booths to make room for new artists at Indian Market. Many immediately protested, arguing that these top artists were the reason many collectors came to Indian Market in the first place. In addition, the top artists served as models of artistic creativity and success for the younger artists. Ultimately, the Masters Market failed because few artists wanted to participate and attendance was low. Most importantly, many Pueblo people found the concept offensive. One artist explained that Pueblo people are humble; they don't consider themselves "masters."

PERIPHERAL ACTIVITIES

Buying straight from the artist is at the core of Indian Market's prosperity. An artist sells his or her own work; there are no middle people, dealers, or

A SANTO DOMINGO TRADER SELLS OTHER ARTISTS' JEWELRY AND TEXTILES AT INDIAN MARKET IN 1971. AS OF 1975, ONLY EXHIBITORS SELLING THEIR OWN WORK WERE ADMITTED TO INDIAN MARKET.

traders. This was not always the case. Beginning in the early 1960s and end-ing in the mid-1970s, dealers and traders (some Anglo but mostly Santo Domingo) were allowed to sell Navajo jewelry and rugs at Indian Market. These dealers were asked to leave. In addition, some Anglos sold wares at Indian Market; some were artistic partners to their Indian wives. After com-plaints from the Zuni Crafts Guild and other Indians, SWAIA ruled that no Anglos would be allowed in the booths. In 1977 an Anglo couple sued the association when they were denied entry into the market. The New Mexico Human Rights Commission ruled in SWAIA's favor, largely based upon the historical precedent of the portal and the plaza being the focus of Indian commerce in Santa Fe for three centuries.

When denied entry, many nonqualifying individuals moved to the fringes of the market, setting up unauthorized booths. SWAIA posted signs showing the limits of the market but otherwise left the squatters alone. In 1980, 220 squatters were counted. According to Don Owen, former SWAIA executive director, squatters with "camp stoves with hot grease set up on sidewalks . . . and [antique Indian art] dealers from Gallup, Los Angeles, and Fresno set up in front of Sears [Lincoln Ave.]." In 1980 SWAIA put up portable toilets on Sheridan Avenue near the Fine Arts Museum, hoping to discourage the squatters; the effort was unsuccessful. In 1982 the city enacted an ordinance prohibiting vendors other than Indian Market participants from selling on city property, such as city sidewalks and parking lots.

But in the years since, opportunists have found myriad ways to skirt the prohibition. Some entities, such as Santa Fe County and the Institute of American Indian Arts (IAIA), allow nonmarket vendors to set up outside their buildings—just beyond the official marked boundaries of the market. Opportunists also sell wares on side streets and in hotel ballrooms. Many sellers are Indian Market applicants who did not qualify for the show. Some are Huichol, Tarahumara, Bolivian, and Mayan indigenous peoples selling their own traditional wares. Others are dealers, both scrupulous and unscrupulous. Meanwhile, every store around the plaza holds sales, puts on special displays, and keeps longer hours to take advantage of the extra business during market week. Southwest-style gift shops near the plaza also sell cheap knockoffs of Indian art.

ZUNI POTTER RANDY NAHOHAI, 2010.

INDIAN MARKET 1971.

Interlopers even make it inside the boundaries of Indian Market. Anglo dealers and some artists walk through the plaza throngs selling Navajo kachina dolls, earrings, concha belts, and bracelets. Vendors wheel carts full of *biscochitos*, tamales, and chile through the crowd. There is also a burgeoning trade in supplies that Indian artists need, such as feathers and cut and polished stones. Artists frequently trade for and buy one another's work.

During the two weeks prior to Indian Market, every evening is filled with gallery and museum openings, auctions, concerts, film showings, fundraisers, and antique tribal art shows. The Santa Fe Convention Center and El Museo Cultural de Santa Fe host ethnic and tribal art shows and a large antique Indian art show. The summer flea market in Tesuque is crowded with new vendors and customers in town for Indian Market. Restaurants and hotels run at capacity, with most restaurants extending their hours to handle the throngs of visitors.

THREE GENERATIONS OF THE GROWING THUNDER-FOGARTY FAMILY ENJOY INDIAN MARKET IN 2010.

Indian Market usually falls within a week or so of the annual feast days at Santa Clara and Zia pueblos. Both celebrations are well attended, with an influx of tourists and visitors from Santa Fe in for the market. Many artists hold their own openings before the market. Toni Roller and family hosted a Margaret Tafoya family show at her studio and home at Santa Clara from 1992 to 2005. Lonnie Vigil thanked his friends and buyers with a feast at his home on the Wednesday before market from 1996 to 2004.

ENSURING HIGH STANDARDS

In the early 1970s, SWAIA's executive secretary sent out invitations to participate in Indian Market. People showed up on Saturday morning, paid a booth fee, and took a space. In 1973 the booth fee was $5. By the end of the decade it was $65. (In 2012 fees were $650 for a ten-by-ten-foot booth and $400 for a five-by-ten.)

In 1977 SWAIA decided to make Indian Market into a juried show. "This would be an effective way to restrict the market to qualified craftsmen and eliminate the mass-produced products and also the dealers," according to former executive director Don Owen. In addition, the market had expanded to fill all available space and needed to limit its size. SWAIA believed that jurying the show would remove the dealers and the "corn bead ladies," making more room for authentic Native artists and craftspeople.

In the same year, SWAIA established a standards committee to evaluate each booth for "quality, authenticity, and cultural identity." The committee scored each booth on a rating scale of 1 (highest) to 4 (lowest). Only booths earning 1s and 2s were supposed to be invited the next year. According to Owen, the "art cops" also formed in the late 1970s. They patrolled the plaza during the weekend, making sure that only artists registered with SWAIA were selling, that the objects for sale were actually made by the artists selling them, and that exhibitors were selling only what they had listed on their applications, in those categories for which they were approved. (In 2009 SWAIA began using digital images to monitor artists and their work.)

As Indian Market grew, more and more non-Pueblo artists began to participate. In 1985 a nonsouthwestern artist won best of show. Ranker spread between Southwest Indians and those from outside the area. "Let them start their own market," one artist told me. "We started this for ourselves." To acknowledge the roots of Indian Market as a Pueblo market, in 1992 SWAIA tenured approximately 570 veteran Pueblo artists, automatically qualifying them for all successive markets.

Today's Indian Market takes a year to develop, plan, and organize. Artist applications go out in October and must be returned by January. (For the 2012 show, SWAIA received nearly two thousand applications.) A volunteer panel of experts evaluates every applicant for artistic creativity and quality of workmanship. After acceptance letters go out in March, the SWAIA office is flooded with phone calls and e-mails from disappointed applicants. Staff members patiently explain why certain applications were rejected. (Many applicants who are rejected initially go on to be accepted and to win awards in later markets.) Above all else, SWAIA procedures and rules are designed to have the highest art quality included in Indian Market. Quality, of course, has multiple meanings. So while aesthetics is a primary means for jurying artists, materials and technologies continue to be of critical importance too.

The rules and standards for today's Indian Market fill hundreds of pages. The rules define eleven art classifications. They describe specific tribal styles as well as nontribal art forms such as painting and sculpture. The rules detail what is and is not traditional; define pottery techniques, shapes, and forms;

AT THE BEST OF SHOW JUDGING IN 2011, SCULPTOR GEORGE RIVERA (POJOAQUE) EXPLAINS TO OTHER JUDGES THE QUALI-TIES OF A WINNING PIECE.

and define every judging classification. Generally, the rules favor traditional and contemporary handcrafted items. For example, Native materials and firing techniques are strongly encouraged in pottery. Electric-kiln-fired and double-fired pieces are accepted, as long as they are labeled as such. However, they are downgraded in judging and are judged in the nontraditional categories.

SWAIA uses the extensive rules in part to remove buyers' anxieties. The rules help control quality and create an atmosphere of honest representation of artworks. SWAIA guarantees authenticity, thereby also increasing the comfort level of buyers. Certainly, SWAIA wants to include only the best artists to maintain Indian Market's reputation for quality. At the same time, the association does not want to stifle creativity.

INDIAN MARKET
PREVIEW, 2011.

Through 1971, all judging was done in the booths on Saturday morning. But as the number of booths grew, this system was no longer feasible. So in 1972 all entries for judging were taken by 8:30 a.m. Saturday to the patio of the Palace of the Governors, where judging was done privately. By all accounts, this process was a disaster because pieces were removed from artists' booths and were not returned until the late afternoon. Many artists chose to keep their pieces available for sale rather than enter them for judging.

In 1975 judging was moved to La Fonda Hotel, where it could be done with more privacy and more time. Entries were accepted on Friday afternoon, judged that evening, and redistributed to the artists beginning at 6:00 a.m. on Saturday. In 1982 the judging format was changed again. This time entries were taken on Thursday and judging took place on Friday.

In 1984 SWAIA held its first member-only preview of the award winners—so everyone would know who the winners were before the market opened. The event turned the mezzanine of La Fonda into a zoo, as award-winning pieces were laid out on tables and a line of viewers inched by for four hours. Judges stood nearby to explain why certain pieces had won awards.

The preview put additional emphasis on winning. People were eager to know the prizewinning pieces and to purchase them. (Some accused the judges, who were predominantly dealers at this time, of purchasing prizewinners before the opening of the market.)

As the market grew and La Fonda became more crowded with entries, it became difficult to lay out the hundreds of pieces of jewelry, pots, paintings, sculpture, and textiles. So in 1990 SWAIA moved the judging and preview from La Fonda to the Sweeney Convention Center (now the Santa Fe Convention Center). Entries were taken from 11:00 a.m. to 6:00 p.m. on Thursday, judging was all day Friday, and Friday evening was the preview. After leaving the Convention Center from 2006 to 2008 due to the construction of a new building, judging and previews are now back there. Receiving has been moved to Wednesday, judging is on Thursday, and previews are on Friday.

One gets the first whiff of Indian Market's greatness at receiving. The process is facilitated by about two hundred dedicated volunteers, many of whom have been helping the organization for many decades. They arrive several hours early for extensive training. Then they process the roughly thirteen hundred pieces (one or two from each artist) for judging.

Judging begins early Thursday morning and takes most of the day. The judges are art dealers, collectors, museum curators, and Indian artists—seventy-eight in all. They are chosen for their knowledge of Indian art and might have a particular expertise in pottery, jewelry, sculpture, or painting.

A 2010 SWAIA POSTER FEATURED ARTIST GERONIMA MONTOYA (OHKAY OWINGEH), AN INDIAN MARKET PARTICIPANT SINCE THE 1930S.

Being asked to serve as a judge carries some prestige. In 1992, there were twenty-six judges: in 2011 there were seventy. There has been a considerable effort to bring new judges into the mix, including those outside of the Native arts field.

The judges work in teams of no less than three. In the larger classifications of jewelry and pottery, three teams of three work their way through the entries. The judges attempt to balance their different frames of reference, ultimately interpreting the work as containers of cultural value, objects of aesthetic achievement, and art to decorate homes.

INNOVATION

Indian Market judging classifications have changed as Indian art has changed. For example, with the 1962 arrival in Santa Fe of the IAIA, new art forms followed. Indian Market rules quickly changed to accommodate these forms. IAIA brought an infusion of sculpture and nontraditional painting entries into Indian Market.

Most famously, Allan Houser trained many sculpture students, and their work necessitated rewriting the rules for sculpture entries and the eventual establishment of a sculpture classification. The rules for sculpture entries had been slightly altered in the late 1960s when Helen Cordero and Domancia Cordero won awards for their clay sculptures. However, Bob Haozous in 1971 permanently changed the category when he won a first prize for a mahogany wood sculpture. The following year Haozous entered a stone sculpture that permanently changed Indian Market art classifications. In Haozous's first win he was judged in the category that included pottery figurines; in the following year he was judged against Hopi katsina figures. The change has been so conclusive that now sculpture is often spoken of as a "traditional" art form.

In 1975 and again in 1976 Native artist Fritz Scholder offered a $1,000 special award to create a new contemporary painting category. Scholder wanted to judge the entrants alone, but SWAIA's board of directors rejected his offer. A number of Indian artists also objected, saying "Fritz Scholder had no regard for the traditional Indian artists and had publicly ridiculed their work," recalled artist and SWAIA board member Geronima Montoya.

The emotional outpouring directed against Scholder, and by extension against the IAIA, reflected SWAIA's long relationship with local Pueblo communities and its endorsement of the flat "traditional" style of painting. When contemporary painter Harry Fonseca (interestingly, a non-IAIA artist) won the award for best painting in 1980, the tacit constraints were finally lifted, allowing participation of all types of painters.

BEST OF SHOW POT, 1984, CRE-
ATED BY JODY FOLWELL (SANTA
CLARA) AND BOB HAOZOUS
(CHIRICAHUA APACHE).

Change came rapidly in the 1980s as the national contexts for Native-produced art continued to expand. Jewelry designer Gail Bird and her partner, jeweler Yazzie Johnson, forever changed the perceptions of Native jewelers with their best of show win in 1981. Just a few years earlier, their piece (which was neither silver nor turquoise) had been rejected for exhibition.

In 1984 a green-slipped kiva pot with incised cowboy and Indian figures won best of show. The pot was traditional because it was manufactured by Jody Folwell in the time-honored methods of Santa Clara Pueblo. It was nontraditional because of the designs and the green color and further because sculptor Bob Haozous, a Chiricahua Apache, had assisted in its design and incising. Its appeal was in its innovation as social commentary, with all the cowboys falling upside down off their horses and the Indians riding victoriously around them.

The judging that year was tense. The judges split their votes between the green pot and a beautiful and meticulous miniature melon bowl by Nancy Youngblood. Some judges praised the innovation of the Folwell/Haozous piece while decrying the thought of giving "another prize to another black pot" (the Youngblood piece). Other judges bemoaned the cowboy and Indian piece, saying they had no desire "to encourage more green pots," which they insisted were unsalable. The green pot created a dilemma for the judges because under the rules it was a traditional pot (in terms of materials and techniques); only its color and decoration were nontraditional. But given the perfection of its execution, along with the evocative design, the green pot won.

The victory of "Cowboys and Indians" influenced what would be accepted at subsequent markets. Green pots and those decorated in realist styles or depicting messages of social commentary were not changes anticipated or encouraged by Indian Market officials. But rules were flexible, and the following year green-slipped pots were everywhere at Indian Market and were widely accepted.

The rapid infusion of nontraditional art forms and (professionally trained) artists has created something of a backlash. It has actually helped foster a resurgence in the traditional arts. When Joyce Growing Thunder Fogarty won the first of her three best of shows in 1985, it was for an entirely traditional art form, beadwork

Today, the tension between traditional and nontraditional forms is less intense. When Jeremy Fry, a Passamaquoddy basket maker, won in 2011 there was no talk of whether his work was too traditional or contemporary. There was only admiration for the strikingly made piece.

PREVIEW

The Indian Market preview is now attended by thousands of people. Some carefully take notes to map out which booths they will visit first the next day. Others look for new and undiscovered artists. Some award winners stand near their pieces at the preview and enthusiastically receive the admiring throngs; others are overwhelmed by the attention. All are humbled by the experience of winning and the unbridled display of admiration.

Following the preview, people pour out of the convention center and visit the myriad of gallery openings, stopping to say hello to friends and acquaintances. Downtown streets are closed to vehicle traffic, and the booths are erected. Many artists install backboards, shelves, and pedestals in their booths on Friday.

SHOWTIME

On Saturday morning, beginning at 5:00 a.m., hundreds of vehicles carrying exhibitors and their works descend on the plaza area. Drivers weave their

OPPOSITE
POTTER JASON GARCIA OF SANTA CLARA DISPLAYS A PIECE IN 2011. HE TAKES HIS INFLUENCES FROM HIS COMMUNITY AS WELL AS FROM THE WORLD OF COMIC BOOKS AND POP MUSIC.

ARTISTS UNLOAD WORK AT THEIR BOOTHS AT 5:30 ON SATURDAY MORNING, 2010.

way to the booths, quickly unload, and park their cars. After months of work, pieces are ready to be shown and sold. The exhibitors are brilliantly dressed and coiffed. They gird themselves for the crowds and for the praise and criticism of thousands. Their spouses, children, and friends stand ready to help with the frenzy of admirers and questions.

About fifty artists typically sell out by noon. Others might sell little or nothing all day. Many exhibitors make between 40 and 100 percent of their yearly income at Indian Market. Some tally earnings of six figures annually, but most earn far less. But even if sales are low, exhibitors know there are gallery owners and curators a-plenty in the crowd. They might make additional purchases in the next week or month.

BEYOND INDIAN MARKET

Face-to-face at Indian Market was once the only way to communicate with most exhibitors. Just a few decades ago, not every artist had a telephone. Letters to them often went unanswered. In the twenty-first century, cell phones, the Internet, and artist websites have drastically changed that picture. Collectors now talk with artists year-round. In addition, artists increasingly understand the need to be salespeople too—calling, e-mailing, and texting their collectors; visiting them throughout the year; and sending updates and previews of the new work they are producing for Indian Market.

Indeed, the real currency of Indian Market is relationships. As the proverbial cacaphony of people, Indian Market is an honest, viable, up-to-the-minute report on who Indian people are today. Certainly, people can enter Indian Market with powerful misplaced images—on both sides of the booth. But it takes only a few minutes of people-watching or admiring the variety of art to have such preconceived stereotypes smashed.

At Indian Market, visitors and artists alike are pleased to the find the predictable and unpredictable, change and continuity, tradition and innovation, the new and old side by side. Everyone responds differently to the experience. For some, Indian Market begins as a quiet whisper; for others, as a beautiful, full-throated song.

SELECTED BIBLIOGRAPHY

ARCHIVAL AND UNPUBLISHED SOURCES

American Museum of Natural History, New York
    Spinden Papers
    Object collections and records

Hearst Museum of Anthropology, Berkeley
    Object collections

Museum of Indian Arts and Culture/Laboratory of Anthropology, Santa Fe
    Kenneth Chapman Papers
    Herman Schweizer Correspondence
    Object collections and records

Museum fur Volkerkunde, Berlin
    Object collections

Museum of International Folk Art Library, Santa Fe
    Fred Harvey Papers

New Mexico History Museum, Santa Fe
    J. S. Candelario Collection
    Edgar Hewett Collection
    Photo Archives

New Mexico Museum of Art (Museum of Fine Arts), Santa Fe
    John Sloan files

National Archives, Washington, D.C.
    Record Group 435, Bureau of Indian Affairs

New Mexico State Records Center and Archives, Santa Fe
    Fiesta file
    Jake Gold file
    Southwestern Association on Indian Affairs papers

Rijksmusuem voor Volkerkunde, Leiden

School for Advanced Research, Santa Fe
  Elizabeth White Papers
  Kenneth Chapman Papers
  Object collections and records
  Carl Guthe Field Notebook

Smithsonian Institution Anthropology Department, Washington, D.C.
  Accession and object records
  Object collections

The Autry, Braun Research Library, Los Angeles
  Fred Hinton Papers and Photographs
  Frederick Hodge Papers

Zimmerman Library, University of New Mexico, Albuquerque
  De Huff Papers

PUBLISHED REFERENCES

Aberle, Sophie
1948   *The Pueblo Indians of New Mexico: Their Land, Economy, and Civil Organiza-
          tion.* Memoirs of the American Anthropological Association 70. Menasha, WI:
          American Anthropological Association.

Adkins, Lynn
1983   "Jesse L. Nusbaum and the Painted Desert in San Diego." *Journal of San Diego
          History* 29:86–95.

Amero, Richard
1990   "The Making of the Panama-California Exposition." *Journal of San Diego
          History* 36:1–43.

Austin, Mary
1926   "The Town That Doesn't Want a Chautauqua." *New Republic* 47.
1928   "Indian Arts for Indians." *Survey Graphic* 13(4):381–87.

Ayers, John
1949   "A Soldier's Experience." *New Mexico Historical Review* 24(4):259–66.

Bandelier, Adolph
1966   *The Southwestern Journals of Adolph F. Bandelier* 1880–1882. Edited by
          Charles Lange and Carrol Riley. Albuquerque: University of New Mexico Press.

Bandelier, Adolph, and Edgar Hewett
1937   *Indians of the Rio Grande Valley*. Albuquerque: University of New Mexico.

Batkin, Jonathan
1987   *Pottery of the Pueblos of New Mexico, 1700–1940.* Colorado Springs:
          Colorado Springs Fine Arts Center.
2008   *The Native American Curio Trade in New Mexico*. Santa Fe: Wheelwright
          Museum of the American Indian.

Benedict, Burton
1983   *The Anthropology of World's Fairs: San Francisco's Panama Pacific International Exposition of 1915.* Berkeley: Scolar Press.

Bernstein, Bruce
1993   "The Marketing of Culture: Pottery and Santa Fe's Indian Market." PhD dissertation, University of New Mexico, 1993.
1993   "Indian Fair to Indian Market." *El Palacio* 98:14–20, 47–54.
1994   "Potters and Patrons: The Creation of Pueblo Art Pottery." *American Indian Art* 20:70–80.
1994   "Pueblo Potters, Museum Curators, and Santa Fe's Indian Market." *Expedition* 36:14–23.
1999   "Santa Fe and the Creation of Indian Art: Contexts for the Development and Growth of the Indian Art World of the 1970s." In *Twentieth Century Native American Art: Essays on History and Criticism.* Jackson Rushing, ed. Pp 57–71. London: Routledge Press.
2007   "The Booth Sitters of Indian Market: Maintaining and Creating Authenticity." *American Indian Culture and Research Journal* 31(3): 49–79.
2007   "The Passion of Santa Fe Indian Market: Camping Out, Booth Sitting, and Other Curious Phenomena." *El Palacio* (Summer 2007).

Brand, Stewart
1988   "Indians and the Counterculture, 1960s–1970s." In *Handbook of North American Indians.* Vol. 4: *History of Indian-White Relations.* Wilcomb Washburn, ed. Pp. 570–572. Washington, D.C.: Smithsonian Institution Press.

Brody, J. J.
1971   *Indian Painters and White Patrons.* Albuquerque: University of New Mexico Press.
1989   *Beauty from the Earth: Pueblo Indian Pottery from the University Museum of Archaeology and Anthropology.* Philadelphia: University Museum of Archaeology and Anthropology.
2004   *Mimbres Painted Pottery.* Revised ed. Santa Fe: School of American Research Press.

Bronwen Horton, Sarah
2010   *The Santa Fe Fiesta, Reinvented: Staking Ethno-Nationalist Claims to a Disappearing Homeland.* Santa Fe: School for Advanced Research.

Bryant, Keith
1974   "The Atchison, Topeka and Santa Fe Railway and the Development of the Taos and Santa Fe Art Colonies." *Western Historical Quarterly* 9(4):437–53.

Bsumek, Erika Marie
2008   *Indian Made: Navajo Culture in the Marketplace, 1868–1940.* Lawrence: University of Kansas Press.

Bunting, Banbridge
1983   *John Gaw Meem: Southwestern Architect.* Santa Fe: School of American Research.

Bunzel, Ruth
1929   *The Pueblo Potter: A Study of Creative Imagination in Primitive Art.* New York: Columbia University Press, 36.

Burge, Margaret McKittrick
1935   *Contemporary Southwestern Indian Arts and Crafts.* Santa Fe: New Mexico Association on Indian Affairs.

Burton, Henrietta
1936   *The Re-Establishment of the Indians in Their Pueblo Life through the Revival of Their Traditional Crafts: A Study in Home Extension Education*. New York: Teachers College, Columbia University.

Carroll, Terry Lee
1971   "Gallup and Her Ceremonials." PhD dissertation, University of New Mexico.

Chapman, Janet, and Karen Barrie
2008   *Kenneth Milton Chapman: A Life Dedicated to Indian Arts and Artists*. Albuquerque: University of New Mexico Press.

Chapman, Kenneth
1924   "The Indian Fair." *Art and Archaeology* 18(5–6):215–24.
1925   "Address to the Fifth Annual Conference of the Western Association of Art Museum Directors." *El Palacio* 19(1):14–18.
1936   "Roadside Shopping." *New Mexico Magazine* 14(6):20–21, 38–39.
1978   *The Pottery of San Ildefonso Pueblo*. Albuquerque: University of New Mexico Press.

Chauvenet, Beatrice
1983   *Hewett and Friends: A Biography of Santa Fe's Vibrant Era*. Santa Fe: Museum of New Mexico Press.

Dauber, Kenneth
1990   "Pueblo Pottery and the Politics of Regional Identity." *Journal of the Southwest* 32(4):576–96.

D'Emilio, Sandra, and Suzan Campbell
1991   *Visions and Visionaries: The Art and Artists of the Santa Fe Railway*. Salt Lake City: Peregrine Smith Books.

DeHuff, John
1923   The Southwest Indian Fair. *El Palacio* 15(10):173–175.

Dietrich, Margretta
1936   "Old Art in New Forms." *New Mexico Magazine* 14(9):26–27, 56.
1943   *Doing Fine and Thanks a Million*. Santa Fe: NMAIA.
1945   *Hello and Many Lucks*. Santa Fe: NMAIA.
1952   "The History of Indian Market." *Santa Fe New Mexican*, August 29.

Dozier, Edward
1961   Rio Grande Pueblos. In *Perspectives in American Indian Culture Change*. Edward H. Spicer, ed. Pp. 94–186. Chicago: University of Chicago Press.
1964   "The Pueblo Indians of the Southwest." *Current Anthropology* 5(2):79–97.
1966   "Factionalism at Santa Clara Pueblo." *Ethnology* 5:172–85.
1970   *The Pueblo Indians of North America*. New York: Holt, Rinehart and Winston, Inc.

Dutton, Bertha
1944   "Fiesta Dances at the Museum." *El Palacio* 51(9):177.

Eickemeyer, Carl and Eickemeyer, L.
1895   *Among the Pueblo Indians*. New York: Merriam Company.

El Palacio

1914 "Museum and School Share in San Diego's Triumph." *El Palacio* 2(2):1–3.

1917 "Museum Notes." *El Palacio* 4(1):101.

1918a "Historic Pageant for Santa Fe." *El Palacio* 5(4):62–63.

 b "Indian Arts Center." *El Palacio* 5(13):239.

 c "Indians and Folk Lore." *El Palacio* 5(17):285–86.

1919 "The Santa Fe Fiesta." *El Palacio* 7(5–6):97–132.

1920a "America's Supreme Artist." *El Palacio* 8(3–4):86–87.

 b "Fine Exhibit of Pottery." *El Palacio* 8(7–8):217.

1922a "Official Program of the Santa Fe Fiesta." *El Palacio* 13(4):47–52.

 b "The Southwest Indian Fair." 13(8): 93–97. *El Palacio.*

1923a "Premium List of the Southwest Indian Fair." *El Palacio* 15(2):23–27.

 b "The Southwest Indian Fair." *El Palacio* 13(8):93–97.

 c "Santa Fe Fiesta and Indian Fair." *El Palacio* 15(6):100–104.

1924a "The Santa Fe Fiesta." *El Palacio* 16(2):43.

 b "The Santa Fe Fiesta." *El Palacio* 16(7):109–15.

 c "The Santa Fe Fiesta and Indian Fair." 17(6–7):125–81.

1925 "The 1925 Fiesta." *El Palacio* 19(5):88–98, 107–117.

1926a "The Indian Fair." *El Palacio* 21(3–5):154–55.

 b "The Santa Fe Fiesta 1926." *El Palacio* 21(4–6):73–105, 123–25.

 c "Summer Work of the School of American Research." *El Palacio* 21(2):39–45.

 d "Southwest Indian Fair 1926." *El Palacio* 20(10):204–12.

1927 "The Indian Fair." *El Palacio* 23(13):343–346.

1928 "Santa Fe Fiesta." *El Palacio* 25(8–11):183.

Fergusson, Erna

1936 "Crusade from Santa Fe." *North American Review* 242:376–87.

1940 *Our Southwest*. New York: Alfred Knopf.

Fewkes, Jesse Walter

1914 "Archaeology of the Lower Mimbres Valley, New Mexico." *Smithsonian Miscellaneous Collections* 63(10):1–60.

1919 "Designs on Prehistoric Hopi Pottery." In *Thirty-Third Annual Report of the Bureau of American Ethnology* 1911–12. Washington D.C.: Bureau of American Ethnology.

1923 "Designs of Prehistoric Pottery from the Mimbres Valley, New Mexico." *Smithsonian Miscellaneous Collections* 74(6):1–47.

1924 "Additional Designs on Prehistoric Mimbres Pottery." *Smithsonian Miscellaneous Collections* 76(8):1–46.

Fowler, Don

1989 "Harvard vs. Hewett: The Contest for Control of Southwestern Archaeology, 1904–1930." Paper presented at the Eighty-Eighth Annual Meeting of the American Anthropological Association, Washington, D.C.

Frost, Richard

1980 "The Romantic Inflation of Pueblo Culture." *American West.* 17(1):4–9, 56–60.

Garmhausen, Winona

1988 *History of Indian Arts Education in Santa Fe*. Santa Fe: Sunstone Press.

Glassberg, David

1990 *American Historical Pageantry: The Uses of Tradition in the Early Twentieth Century*. Chapel Hill: University of North Carolina Press.

Grattan, Mary
1980 *Mary Colter: Builder upon the Red Earth*. Flagstaff, AZ: Northland Press.

Gratz, Kathleen
1976 Origins of the Tesuque Rain God. *El Palacio* 82(3):3–8.

Grimes, Ronald
1976 *Symbol and Conquest*. Ithaca, NY: Cornell University Press.

Gritton, Joy
1991 The Institute of American Indian Arts: A Convergence of Ideologies. In *Shared Visions: Native American Painters and Sculptors in the Twentieth Century*. Margaret Archuleta and Rennard Strickland, eds. Pp. 22–29. Phoenix: Heard Museum.

Guthe, Carl
1925 *Pueblo Pottery Making: A Study at the Village of San Ildefonso*. New Haven, CT: Yale University Press.

Halseth, Odd
1926 "The Revival of Pueblo Pottery Making." *El Palacio* 21(6):135–154.

Harvey, Byron
1963 "The Fred Harvey Collection 1899–1963." *Plateau* 36(2):33–53.

Hedges, Ken, and Alfred Dittert, Jr.
1984 *Heritage in Clay: The 1912 Pueblo Pottery Collections of Wesley Bradfield and Thomas S. Dozier*. San Diego: Museum of Man.

Hewett, Edgar Lee
1922a "First Indian Fair at Santa Fe." *El Palacio* 13(1):12.
1922b "The Southwest Indian Fair." *El Palacio* 13(4):93–97.
1923 "My Neighbors the Pueblo Indians." *El Palacio* 15(8):123–34.
1925 "A Proposed Indian Theater in Santa Fe." *Papers of the School of American Research*, n.s. no. 8.
1930 *Ancient Life in the American Southwest*. New York: Bobbs Merrill.

Hill, W. W.
1982 *An Ethnography of Santa Clara Pueblo New Mexico*. Albuquerque: University of New Mexico.

Hinsley, Curtis
1986 "Edgar Lee Hewett and the School of American Research in Santa Fe 1906–1912." In *American Archaeology: A Celebration of the Society of American Archaeology 1935–1985*. David Meltzer, Don Fowler, and Jeremy Sabloff, eds. Pp. 217–233. Washington, D.C.: Smithsonian Institution Press.
1990 "The World as Marketplace: Commodification of the Exotic at the World's Columbian Exposition, Chicago, 1893." In *Exhibiting Cultures: The Poetics and Politics of Museum Display*. Ivan Karp and Steven Lavine, eds. Pp. 344–365. Washington, D.C.: Smithsonian Institution Press.

Jacobs, Margaret
1999 *Engendered Encounters: Feminism and Pueblo Cultures, 1879–1934*. Lincoln: University of Nebraska Press.

Johnson, William Templeton
1916   "The Santa Fe of the Future." *El Palacio* 3(3):10–31.

Kandarian, Sally, and Helen Hardin
1976   "Indian Market at Santa Fe." *American Indian Art* 1(4):32–33, 58–59.

Kidder, Alfred
1925   *Pueblo Pottery Making: A Study at the Village of San Ildefonso.* New Haven, CT: Yale University Press.

La Farge, Oliver
1959   *Santa Fe: The Autobiography of a Southwestern Town.* Norman: University of Oklahoma.

La Farge, Oliver, and John Sloan
1931   *Introduction to American Indian Art.* 1931. Reprint, Glorieta, NM: Rio Grande Press, 1979

LaFree, Betty
1974   *Santa Clara Pottery Today.* Albuquerque: University of New Mexico Press.

Larson, Robert
1968   *New Mexico's Quest for Statehood* 1846–1912. Albuquerque: University of New Mexico Press.

Lummis, Charles
1892   *A Tramp across the Continent.* New York: Charles Scribner's Sons.
1893   *The Land of Poco Tiempo.* New York: Charles Scribner's Sons.

Manchester, A. D.
1982   "Couriers, Dudes, and Touring Cars: The Legend of Indian Detours." *New Mexico Magazine* 60(6):39–41, 44, 46, 48–49.

Marriott, Alice
1948   *Maria: The Potter of San Ildefonso.* Norman: University of Oklahoma.

Maxwell Museum of Anthropology
1974   *Seven Families in Pueblo Pottery.* Albuquerque: University of New Mexico Press.

McLuhan, T. C.
1985   *Dreamtracks: The Railroad and the American Indian, 1890–1930.* New York: Harry Abrams, Inc.

Miller, Mike
1985   "New Mexico's Role in the Panama-California Exposition of 1915." *El Palacio* 91(2):13–17.

Nusbaum, Rosemary
1980   *Tierra Dulce: Reminiscences from the Jesse Nusbaum Papers.* Santa Fe: Sunstone Press.

Ortiz, Alfonso
1969   *The Tewa World: Space, Time, Being, and Becoming in a Pueblo Society.* Chicago: University of Chicago Press.
1994   "The Dynamics of Pueblo Cultural Survival." In *North American Indian Anthropology: Essays on Society and Culture.* Raymond J. Demallie and Alfonso Ortiz, eds. Pp. 296–307. Norman: University of Oklahoma Press.

Ortiz, Alfonso, ed.
1972   *New Perspectives on the Pueblos*. Albuquerque: University of New Mexico Press.
1979   *Southwest*. Vol. 9 of *Handbook of North American Indians*. Washington, D.C.: Smithsonian Institution Press.

Otis, Raymond
1931   *Indian Art of the Southwest: An Exposition of Methods and Practices*. Santa Fe: NMAIA.

Peterson, Susan
1977   *The Living Tradition of Maria Martinez*. Tokyo: Kodansha International.

Rushing, W. Jackson
1991   "Authenticity and Subjectivity in Post-War Painting: Concerning Herrera, Scholder, and Cannon." In *Shared Visions: Native American Painters and Sculptures in the Twentieth Century*. Margaret Archuleta and Rennard Strickland, eds. Pp. 12–21. Phoenix: Heard Museum.

Rydell, Robert
1984   *All the World's A Fair: Visions of Empire at American International Expositions, 1876–1916*. Chicago: University of Chicago Press.

Sando, Joe
1976   *The Pueblo Indians*. San Francisco: Indian Historian Press.
1992   *Pueblo Nations: Eight Centuries of Pueblo Indian History*. Santa Fe: Clear Light.

Schrader, Robert
1983   *The Indian Arts and Crafts Board: An Aspect of the New Deal Indian Policy*. Albuquerque: University of New Mexico Press.

Schroeder, Gail
1964   San Juan Pottery: Methods and Incentives. *El Palacio* 71(1):45–51.

Sheppard, Carl
1988   *Creator of the Santa Fe Style: Isaac Hamilton Rapp, Architect*. Albuquerque: University of New Mexico Press.

Simmons, Marc
1979   "History of the Pueblos since 1821." In *Handbook of North American Indians*. Vol. 9: *Southwest*. Alfonso Ortiz, ed. Pp. 206–23. Washington, D.C.: Smithsonian Institution Press.

Snow, David
1973   "Some Economic Considerations of Historic Rio Grande Pueblo Pottery." In *The Changing Ways of Southwestern Indians: A Historic Perspective*. Albert Schroeder, ed. Pp. 55–72. Glorieta, NM: Rio Grande Press.

Southwestern Association on Indian Affairs
1965   "Annual Indian Market and Dances." *Quarterly of the Southwestern Association on Indian Affairs* 2(4):1.
1968   "Indian Wares in a Historic Setting." *Quarterly of the Southwestern Association on Indian Affairs* 5(1–2):1–6.

Spivey, Richard
2003   *The Legacy of Maria Poveka Martinez*. Santa Fe: Museum of New Mexico Press.

Thomas, D. H.

1978   *The Southwestern Indian Detours: The Story of the Fred Harvey/Santa Fe Railway Experiment in "Detourism."* Phoenix: Hunter Publishing.

Trennert, Robert

1987   "Fairs, Expositions, and the Changing Image of Southwestern Indians," 1876–1904. *New Mexico Historical Review* 62:127–50.

Trimble, Stephen

1987   *Talking with the Clay: The Art of Pueblo Pottery*. Santa Fe: School of American Research.

Von Blumenthal, Verra

1919   "Preservation of National Arts." *El Palacio* 7(4):70–73.

Walter, Paul

1924   "The Santa Fe Fiesta of September, 1924." *Art and Archaeology* 18(5–6):181–94.
1947   "Edgar Lee Hewett, Americanist, 1865–1947." *American Anthropologist* 49(2):260–71.

Weigle, Marta

1986   "Civilizers, Art Colonists, Couriers, and Civil Servants: The Role of Women in Popularizing the Native American Southwest, 1902–1940." Paper prepared for the Wenner-Gren Foundation symposium Daughters of the Desert: Women Anthropologists and Students of the Native American Southwest, Tucson, Arizona.
1989   "From Desert to Disney World: The Santa Fe Railway and the Fred Harvey Company Display the Indian Southwest." *Journal of Anthropological Research* 45(1):114–38.
1990   "Southwest Lures: Innocents Detoured, Incensed Determined." *Journal of the Southwest* 32(4):499–540.
1992   "Exposition and Mediation: Mary Colter, Erna Fergusson, and the Santa Fe/Harvey Popularization of the Native Southwest, 1902–1940." *Frontiers* 12(3):117–50.

Weigle, Marta, and Kyle Fiore

1982   *Santa Fe and Taos: The Writers' Era*. Santa Fe: Ancient City Press.

Weigle, Marta, and Peter White

1988   *The Lore of New Mexico*. Albuquerque: University of New Mexico Press.

Whitman, William

1940   "The San Ildefonso of New Mexico." In *Acculturation in Seven American Indian Tribes*. Ralph Linton ed. Pp. 390–460. New York: D. Appleton-Century.
1947   *The Pueblo Indians of San Ildefonso: A Changing Culture*. Columbia University Contributions to Anthropology 34. New York: Columbia University.

Wilson, Chris

1997   *The Myth of Santa Fe: Creating a Modern Regional Tradition*. Albuquerque: University of New Mexico Press.

ACKNOWLEDGMENTS

THIS BOOK SHARES AUTHORSHIP with many people. There are as many Indian Market stories as there are market-goers. Artists, collectors, volunteers, SWAIA staff and board, and Indian Market goers have provided information in the form of formal and informal interviews. A heartfelt appreciation to each and everyone one of you who sat down with me or merely crossed my line of pen and notepad over the years.

I am particularly indebted to the guidance of the late Alfonso Ortiz and to Marta Weigle and Jerry Brody of the University of New Mexico. A summer Buntin scholarship at the School of Advanced Research helped advance my research. Museum, archives, and library staff have been generous: Stephen Becker, Diane Bird, Tony Chavarria, and Valerie Verzuh of the Museum of Indian Arts and Culture/Laboratory of Anthropology; Daniel Kosharek, and Tomas Jaehn at the Palace of the Governors library and archives; Laura Ellif, Michael Hering, and Laura Holt of the School of Advanced Research; and many other institutions and individuals, including, Tailinh Agoyo, Jonathan Batkin, Peter Bols, Pieter Hovens, Jonathan King, Joe Traugott, and Mary Lyn Salvador.

My knowledge and understanding of the history and circumstances of Indian Market have been shaped and sharpened through interviews with many people, most notably, Rex Arrowsmith, Gail Bird, Jane Buchsbaum, Maria Chabot, Anita Da, Rick Dillingham, Bertha Dutton, Majorie Lambert, Lucy Lowden, Geronima Montoya, Tessie Naranjo, Don Owen, Al Packard, Ruth Schultz, John Torres Nez, Sallie Wagner, and Letta Wofford.

The Museum of New Mexico Press has provided superb guidance: editorial director Mary Wachs, art director David Skolkin and designer Jason Valdez, and director Anna Gallegos. Peg Goldstein edited the manuscript, and Gregory Pleshaw provided invaluable guidance and editing as well.

As always, I am indebted to the indulgence and intelligence of my partner and wife Landis Smith.

My deepest gratitude is to the artists of Indian Market. While over the years they have shared their thoughts and aspirations with me, I take full responsibility for my interpretation and use of their comments. As a scholar one learns to perform research in libraries, archives, collections, or interviews. Artists have generously shared with me their perspectives that continue to clarify and enhance what I read and taught me through words and their art the true meanings and values of Native art and Indian Market. To the artists of Indian Market, past and present, I dedicate this book.

CREDITS

Back cover: Courtesy of SWAIA, photos by Kitty Leaken

Title page: Courtesy Division of Anthropology, American Museum of Natural History, 50.2/4140.

Page 6: Courtesy of SWAIA, photo by Chris Corrie

Page 9: Private collection.

Page 11: Courtesy of SWAIA, photo by Chris Corrie

Page 13: Courtesy of SWAIA, photo by Tony Bonanno

Page 14: Courtesy of SWAIA, photo by Kitty Leaken

Page 15: Photo by the author.

Page 16: Fray Angelico Chavez History Library (NMHM/DCA), AC 201-1-12.

Page 19: Palace of the Governors Photo Archives (NMHM/DCA), 014288.

Page 20: Palace of the Governors Photo Archives (NMHM/DCA), 001500.

Page 22: Palace of the Governors Photo Archives (NMHM/DCA), 23317.

Page 24: Courtesy Museum of Indian Arts and Culture/Laboratory of Anthropology (DCA), 1878/12. Photo by Blair Clark.

Page 29: Courtesy of the Library of Congress, Photograph by Edward Curtis, 12314-B.

Page 31: Division of Anthropology, American Museum of Natural History, 50.1/3498.

Page 31: National Anthropology Archives, Smithsonian Institution, BAE GN 2097 A, Photo by Adam Clark Vroman.

Page 32: Private collection.

Page 35: Palace of the Governors Photo Archives (NMHM/DCA), 200110. Photo by Karl Moon.

Page 38: Courtesy of Museum of Indian Arts/Laboratory of Anthropology (DCA), 22020/11 and 11171/12. Photo by Blair Clark.

Page 38: Courtesy of Museum of Indian Arts/Laboratory of Anthropology (DCA), 1769/12. Photo by Blair Clark.

Page 39: Enhanced photo of Tsirge rock panel from El Palacio (Haynes) 1918:234.

Page 40: Palace of the Governors Photo Archives (NMHM/DCA), 060395. Photo by Jesse Nusbaum.

Page 41: Palace of the Governors Photo Archives (NMHM/DCA), 147992. Photo by Jesse Nusbaum.

Page 42: Courtesy of Museum of Indian Arts/Laboratory of Anthropology (DCA), photo by Blair Clark.

Page 43: Courtesy of Museum of Indian Arts/Laboratory of Anthropology (DCA), 18798/12. Photo by Blair Clark.

Page 44: Courtesy of Museum of Indian Arts/Laboratory of Anthropology (DCA), 18702/12. Photo by Blair Clark.

Page 46: Palace of the Governors Photo Archives (NMHM/DCA), 52378.

Page 48: Palace of the Governors Photo Archives (NMHM/DCA), 06448. Photo by Jesse Nusbaum.

Page 50: Palace of the Governors Photo Archives (NMHM/DCA), 10902.

Page 52: Palace of the Governors Photo Archives (NMHM/DCA), 52582.

Page 53: Courtesy of Museum of Indian Arts/Laboratory of Anthropology (DCA), 701/12. Photo by Blair Clark.

Page 57: Courtesy of New Mexico Records and Archives Center, 23929, Margretta Dietrich Collection.

Page 58: Fray Angelico Chavez History Library (NMHM/DCA), 201-1-12.

Page 59: Palace of the Governors Photo Archives (NMHM/DCA), 98340.

Page 61: Courtesy of New Mexico Records and Archives Center, 23925, Margretta Dietrich Collection.

Page 61: Palace of the Governors Photo Archives (NMHM/DCA), 042256.

Page 64: Palace of the Governors Photo Archives (NMHM/DCA), lantern slide 48.

Page 67: Palace of the Governors Photo Archives (NMHM/DCA), 52594.

Page 68: Palace of the Governors Photo Archives (NMHM/DCA), 117985.

Page 69: Private collection.

Page 70: Palace of the Governors Photo Archives (NMHM/DCA), 117818.

Page 72: Courtesy School of Advanced Research, AC02:8331. Photo by Martha White.

Page 74: Chapman Collection, Archives, Courtesy of Museum of Indian Arts and Culture/Laboratory of Anthropology, (DCA) 89KCO.024. Photo by Blair Clark.

Page 78: Chapman Collection, Archives, Courtesy of Museum of Indian Arts and Culture/Laboratory of Anthropology, (DCA) 89KCO.024.2. Photo by Blair Clark.

Page 80: Palace of the Governors Photo Archives (NMHM/DCA), 151535.

Page 84: Gilcrease Museum, Tulsa, OK, 0237.565.

Page 86: Denver Public Library, Western History Collection, US Indian Services, X-30181.

Page 86: Chapman Collection, Archives. Courtesy of Museum of Indian Arts and Culture/Laboratory of Anthropology, (DCA), 89KCO.027. Photo by Blair Clark.

Page 87: Chapman Collection, Archives. Courtesy of Museum of Indian Arts and Culture/Laboratory of Anthropology, (DCA), 89KCO.024.1. Photo by Blair Clark.

Page 88: Palace of the Governors Photo Archives (NMHM/DCA), 004273. Photo by T. Harmon Parkhurst.

Page 90, 91: Courtesy School for Advanced Research, 91:2566.

Page 94: Palace of the Governors Photo Archives (NMHM/DCA), 069973.

Page 98: Palace of the Governors Photo Archives (NMHM/DCA), 117687.

Page 99: Courtesy of Museum of Indian Arts and Culture/Laboratory of Anthropology, (DCA) P19404/12. Photo by Blair Clark.

Page 100: Palace of the Governors Photo Archives (NMHM/DCA), 106994. Photo by Byrd C. Hazelton.

Page 102: Palace of the Governors Photo Archives (NMHM/DCA), 041392, Photo by Robert H. Martin.

Page 104: Palace of the Governors Photo Archives (NMHM/DCA), 30475, Margretta Dietrich Collection.

Page 105: Palace of the Governors Photo Archives (NMHM/DCA), 069979. Photo by T. Harmon Parkhurst.

Page 108: Private collection.

Page 109: Courtesy of SWAIA.

Page 111: Courtesy of SWAIA.

Page 112: Palace of the Governors Photo Archives (NMHM/DCA), 190688.

Page 114: Courtesy of SWAIA.

Page 115: Photo by the author.

Page 115: Courtesy of SWAIA, photo by Julien McRoberts.

Page 116: Courtesy of SWAIA, photo by Chris Corrie.

Page 117: Palace of the Governors Photo Archives (NMHM/DCA), 190706.

Page 118: Courtesy of SWAIA, photo by Julien McRoberts.

Page 119: Palace of the Governors Photo Archives (NMHM/DCA), 1900710.

Page 120: Courtesy of SWAIA, photo by Sara Stathas.

Page 121: Courtesy of SWAIA, photo by Chris Corrie.

Page 122: Palace of the Governors Photo Archives (NMHM/DCA), 132581.

Page 123: Courtesy of SWAIA, photo by Roger Raguso.

Page 125: Courtesy of SWAIA, photo by Kitty Leaken.

Page 126: Courtesy of SWAIA BB??

Page 128: Courtesy of SWAIA, photo by Toba Tucker.

Page 130: Courtesy of SWAIA.

Page 132: Courtesy of SWAIA, photo by M. Kane.

Page 133: Courtesy of SWAIA, photo by Julien McRoberts.

INDEX

Page numbers in italics refer to illustrations.

Project editor: Mary Wachs
Copyediting: Peg J. Goldstein
Design and production: David Skolkin
Layout and cover illustration by Jason Valdez
Composition: Set in New Caledonia
Manufactured in Canada
10 9 8 7 6 5 4 3 2 1

Library of Congress Cataloging-in-Publication Data

Bernstein, Bruce.
Santa Fe Indian market : a history of native arts and the marketplace / by Bruce Bernstein.
p. cm.
Includes bibliographical references and index.
ISBN 978-0-89013-548-8 (pbk. : alk. paper)
1. Indian art—New Mexico—Santa Fe—History. 2. Indians of North America—Commerce—New Mexico—Santa Fe—History. 3. Markets—New Mexico—Santa Fe—History. 4. Tourism—New Mexico—Santa Fe—History. 5. Santa Fe (N. M.)—Social life and customs. I. Title.
E78.N65B39 2012
978.9'56--dc23
2012014672

Title page spread: Gauche on paper, Oqwa Pi (Abel Sanchez), San Ildefonso, purchased by Amelia White at the 1931 Indian Fair and donated to the American Museum of Natural History in 1937.

Museum of New Mexico Press
Post Office Box 2087
Santa Fe, New Mexico 87504
www.mnmpress.org